THE MODERN WORLD
GENERAL EDITOR: C. H. C. BLOUNT

INDONESIA

BY
MALCOLM CALDWELL

OXFORD UNIVERSITY PRESS
1968

Oxford University Press, Ely House, London W.1

GLASGOW NEW YORK TORONTO MELBOURNE WELLINGTON
CAPE TOWN SALISBURY IBADAN NAIROBI LUSAKA ADDIS ABABA
BOMBAY CALCUTTA MADRAS KARACHI LAHORE DACCA
KUALA LUMPUR HONG KONG TOKYO

PRINTED IN GREAT BRITAIN BY
NORTHUMBERLAND PRESS LIMITED
GATESHEAD

CONTENTS

LIST OF PLATES

Cover photograph: Part of the magnificent Buddhist *stupa* of Borobudur, to the north-west of Jogjakarta (second half of the 8th century onwards).

Illustrations are reproduced by courtesy of:
Embassy of the Republic of Indonesia, London (Information Dept): cover photograph and plates 1b, c, and d, 2a and b, 3, 4a and b, 5a, 6b; Camera Press Ltd: plates 1a, 5b, 6a, 7, 8a and b.

I

THE COUNTRY AND THE PEOPLE

INDONESIA's 'confrontation' with Western imperialism has a four hundred and fifty year history. Indeed it was the lure of a group of spice-producing islands in eastern Indonesia that precipitated the age of European expansion; the Spaniards sailing west around the world and the Portuguese sailing east met there, in the Moluccas, in 1521. It is hardly surprising in the light of this that anti-imperialism has played such a prominent part in Indonesia's politics in two decades of independence. Contemporary Indonesian views, unavoidably moulded by the colonial past, cannot but be of significance for the world today in view of the new nation's size, potential, and regional predominance.

Indonesia is a very big country—how big few people in the West seem to appreciate. Superimposed upon Europe, Indonesia would stretch from west of Ireland to east of the Caspian Sea, a total length of 3,400 miles. North to south the maximum breadth is 1,250 miles or, say, the distance from Aberdeen to Madrid. The surface area is 737,000 square miles, nearly eight times that of the United Kingdom, and this puts it among the thirteen largest countries in the world. But Indonesia does not have a compact land area for it is broken up into thousands of islands; with its inland seas included, it covers nearly 4 million square miles (an area greater than the land surface of either China or the United States), thus making the Indonesian archipelago the largest island complex in the world. The islands vary in size from those that are among the world's largest, like Sumatra (roughly as big as Sweden), to uninhabited islets.

In terms of population too Indonesia is a big country.

5

In 1966, with an estimated population of 110 million, it ranked immediately after the big four of China, India, Russia, and America, and ahead of Japan, Pakistan, and Brazil. If the population growth-rate characteristic of recent years persists there may well be nearly 250 million Indonesians by the end of the century. At the moment, 70 per cent are crammed into Java and the small neighbouring islands of Madura, Bali, and Lombok, which taken together make up only 7 per cent of the total land area of Indonesia; Java itself has the greatest population density of any comparable area on earth. Both in population and in area Indonesia accounts for about half the South-East Asian total (South-East Asia consists, in addition to Indonesia, of Burma, Thailand, Laos, Cambodia, Vietnam, Malaysia, Singapore, Portuguese Timor, and the Philippines).

Indonesia tends to predominate in South-East Asia in other ways. It is superbly situated, commanding the routes running east-west from China and Japan to the Indian sub-continent, the Arab world, and the West, and north-south from the South-East Asian mainland to Australasia. It was this favourable position that enabled Indonesian kingdoms to play such a large part in early international commerce in commodities and ideas.

Indonesia has also a bigger and more diversified resource base than any other country in the region. Apart from the precious metals and stones, in which it was at one time thought to be very rich, Indonesia possesses important reserves of petroleum, tin, bauxite (the ore from which aluminium is extracted), manganese (a key metal in the manufacture of steel), coal, iron, and a number of minor, though industrially essential, metals. The known resource base is quite adequate to sustain industrialization.

Culturally, and in a sense politically, Indonesia is widely regarded in the region—even if sometimes reluctantly—as leader of the Malay world, a crescent which includes, besides Indonesia itself, Malaysia, the Philippines, and the southern (largely Muslim) states of Thailand.

Finally, Indonesia's armed forces are (Vietnam at present excepted in all this) the most powerful in South-East Asia; the regular military number over 350,000, a figure substantially greater than all the other countries' forces combined. But it is not simply a question of numbers, for the Indonesian army, navy, and air force have at their disposal really modern weapons and equipment, including, for example, missiles, supplied mainly by the Russians and the Americans. In this respect, Indonesia has profited from her vital strategic location and her pawn value in the Cold War game. At one time, before the right-wing take-over in October 1965, it even looked as if Indonesia might become at least a nominal nuclear power, for China's leaders were contemplating the possibility of assisting Sukarno to obtain and test a nuclear device.

It is quite clear that Indonesia must be by dint of situation and dimensions alone a power to be reckoned with in South-East Asia, the Pacific, and the world. If her leaders can find the key to economic development Indonesia must one day become a *great* power.

Among the people of Indonesia are to be found all types of personality. Nevertheless, the distinctive culture, traditions, and history of the area have stamped themselves upon the people as a whole.

What, then, would be considered characteristically Indonesian? The physical attributes one associates with Indonesians in general are slenderness and lightness of build, gracefulness, moderate stature, straight black hair, and skin coloration ranging from pale yellow to quite dark brown.

If it is legitimate to generalize about temperament

and behaviour, what may be added? Certainly polite-
ness and hospitality. Alongside hospitality, however, goes
moderation in such matters as alcohol; this is enjoined
upon Muslims by their religion, but in this case it is
also in part a reflection of that inner tranquillity which
it is the objective of the traditional culture and value
system to induce.

Many Indonesians today of course wear Western-style
clothes. But traditional dress persists, especially among
the womenfolk, and of course more noticeably in the
countryside than in the cities. Somehow it complements
the features of which we have just spoken. Women wear
an ankle-length *kain* (skirt), a long-sleeved blouse
(*kebaja*), and a stole; this basic costume is subject to
many regional variations. The chief material is *batik*,
the world-famous Indonesian cloth produced by waxing
and dyeing. Traditional male costume consists of a
sarong and an open-necked shirt or high-collared jacket,
with, just possibly, the old-fashioned flat turban (though
nowadays the most common head-dress is the *pitji*—
the black velvet hat associated with President Sukarno
and the nationalist movement). The traditional dress is,
of course, admirably suited to the tropical climate.

Indonesia is wholly tropical, and much the greater
part is equatorial; it is thus the most important equatorial country in the world. The great empires of the
past, notably Srivijaya and Madjapahit, attained the
highest levels of civilization ever achieved so near the
equator. Because of the fragmentation of the land surface, the climate is remarkably homogeneous throughout the country, despite the vast distances involved; the
characteristic features are constant high temperature
with little seasonal variation, high humidity, and heavy
rainfall. The main variations in climate occur as a result
of altitude; mountains and volcanoes are strung across
the archipelago from east to west, and the highest of

them are snow-capped all the year round. There is nothing intrinsically debilitating about the environment, although Djakarta, called Batavia by the Dutch, was at one time known as the graveyard of the East. The main enervating diseases are a product of overcrowding, inadequate sanitation, malnutrition, and other remediable causes. Economic development leading to higher levels of *per capita* income and to all-round improvement in the nation's social capital—housing, drainage, water-supply, medical facilities, and educational provision, for example—would progressively eliminate these obstacles to health and energy. But at the moment with an infant mortality rate nearly four times, and a general mortality rate twice, that of Britain, Indonesia evinces all too clearly the symptoms of economic underdevelopment.

The economic and occupational structure of the country also reflects underdevelopment. The overwhelming majority of Indonesians—85 per cent or so—are rural people, peasant-farmers, and about 60 per cent of national wealth (net domestic product) is generated in the agricultural sector. In contrast, less than 5 per cent of the active population is engaged in agriculture in Britain and 7 per cent in the United States, and in both agriculture contributes only about 4 per cent to national wealth. Rural societies are not rich societies. In 1962 the annual income per head of population in Indonesia was estimated at £24, while that of Britain was £425 and that of America £824.

Although an amazing variety of edible and otherwise useful fruit, vegetables, and cereals flourish in Indonesia, one crop—rice—occupies a unique position. Rice as a staple has several advantages. It is extremely flexible in its soil, water, and climatic requirements. It can, for example, be grown 'dry' along with other crops in slash-and-burn (*swidden*) types of cultivation, or it can be grown 'wet' in inundated fields (*sawah*). It can be grown on soil of rather poor quality as well as on good soil. Yields can be maintained on the same patches of ground over long periods without application of fertilizer. Indonesia's geographical diversity is, therefore, no barrier to general rice production. But it is the flooded padi fields of Java that provide the Indonesian archetype. These terraced rice-fields are both functional and beautiful. The processes of dyking and draining needed to retain and regulate the vital water result in excellent soil conservation practices—American farmers had to be instructed in contour ploughing (the dry land equivalent of rice terraces) when their indiscriminate deep ploughing had transformed huge areas in the mid-West into dust-bowls. The resulting pattern of steps rising up the slopes of hills and volcanoes—sometimes in the latter case to the very brink of the crater—with the glint of water and the distinctive green of the rice crop, is also beautiful.

But the skill and beauty of the rice terraces conceal harsh realities for the Javanese people. From about 4 million at the start of the 19th century, the population of the island has soared to over 70 million. Starting from the most suitable spots—and probably originating in the narrow central neck of the island—intensive *sawah* cultivation of rice subsequently spread north, east, and west until today terraced rice fields occupy virtually every suitable part of Java. The extraordinary thing is that despite continuously more pressing demands on the same soil, yields have not shown any significant tendency to decline. As an area of rice production, Java enjoys a four-fold blessing: the numerous volcanoes which shower the countryside from time to time with deposits rich in plant nutrients; the short swift rivers which carry these deposits away north or south; the gently-sloping bowl-like topography; and the ideal humid climate. But even Java has its limits. What has happened is that as cultivation has intensified there has been less and less rice per person, there being each year more people to feed from a given area of land. Moreover, the desperate need to push cultivation into every conceivable spot has led to a dangerous degree of deforestation. If this trend is not halted and reversed, the age-old and legendary fertility of Java faces disastrous impairment. This crowded hungry island, in fact, is a living microcosm of what the world may, in the absence of conscious human intervention, one day become.

Rice has inherent disadvantages as well as advantages for an economically poor country. The picturesque rural villages of Java, dotted about the undulating landscape of padi fields and terraces, may give an illusion of idyll. But the truth is that irrigated rice cultivation by traditional methods is, in the words of a leading agricultural expert, '. . . without doubt the most time-consuming and laborious of all types of agriculture. Up to ten times as much effort is required to grow an acre of rice as for other field crops. . . .' The cultivation of one hectare of rice requires more than 400 man-days of arduous manual labour (the same area can be managed on a mechanized American farm with seven man-days). Moreover Pierre Gourou, an authority on tropical agriculture, argues that protein, carbohydrate, and fat yields per acre are lower for rice than for wheat. Certainly rice when polished loses much of its original nutritional value. The result is that among the Javanese, as among other rice-eating people, the general level of health is low and working capacity correspondingly limited. On the other hand, research into rice production and processing is at an early stage, and innovations as radical as those that have transformed agriculture in the West are in the offing; already average rice yields in industrialized Japan are considerably higher than those prevalent in Java (the

1961-62 average was 4.7 metric tons per hectare in Japan, 1.8 in Indonesia).

Apart from the sheer quantity problem, however, rice can never afford an adequate diet on its own. Supplementation is essential. There are all kinds of possibilities of introducing scientific rotation with other crops. Already the spectrum of secondary cultivations in Indonesia is astonishing. An official government report produced during the Second World War remarked that Indonesia '. . . held a unique place among tropical countries because of the quantity, variety and excellence of (its) agricultural products.' Some are cultivated in the *sawah* in rotation with rice—an example of this is the soya bean or *kedele*. Others are grown on *tegalan* or unirrigated land, and yet others on *pekarangan*, the grounds around the houses. The importance of these secondary crops is twofold: they help to supplement the diet—in particular by providing proteins and vitamins A and C—and they provide a source of cash income. The major crops in this category include maize, cassava, sweet potatoes, taro, peanuts, red pepper, onions, and a whole host of leafy vegetables, pods, tubers, and fruits. The gardens are remarkable examples of intensive land use though in appearance disorderly and overgrown. The available earth harbours simultaneously low ground-clinging plants (yams, arrowroot, sweet potatoes, and taro), others reaching a greater height (cassava, papaya, banana), and above those still taller bushes and trees (coconut, pomelo, jackfruit, tamarind). An interesting feature of this is that a very large number of the crops now cultivated were introduced from abroad. This is true both of the subsistence sector, to which the Spanish and the Portuguese introduced, among others, the red pepper, maize, sweet potato, cassava, and tobacco, and of the plantation or commercial sector.

The other islands differ in several respects from the

Javanese pattern mainly because of the greater availability of land. *Sawah*, so ubiquitous on Java, dwindles in importance while *swidden* and other more extensive methods prevail. By and large conditions, including climate and soil types, are not so favourable as they are on Java, but the reduced population pressure has enabled the other, or outer, islands to take greater advantage of the commercial crop possibilities. Thus while cassava and sugar are predominantly Javanese products, rubber and copra, major sources along with tin and petroleum of Indonesia's export earnings, are largely grown in the outer islands. The distinctiveness of Java may be grasped by comparing the average density of population per square kilometre there—477—with densities elsewhere: the outer islands as a whole average 19, while for Kalimantan (Indonesian Borneo) the figure is 7.6. Parts of East Java, such as areas in the regency (*kabupaten*) of Malang attain densities up to 2,000 persons per square kilometre. (The world average is 23; the UK figure is 217, and the London figure is 17,000.)

It might appear from these figures that Java's food problems could be solved by moving large numbers of people to the outer islands. Such an option is not, however, available; the operation would be logistically impossible (the annual increase in population on Java is over 1½ million—beyond the capacity of the world's available shipping, let alone Indonesia's). Nor is there actually all that much cultivable land suitable for *sawah* in such islands as Sumatra and Borneo. The cost of opening up what land there is and of settling vast numbers of strangers in virgin territory would in any case be prohibitive. Java, and indeed Indonesia as a whole, must therefore import rice for the foreseeable future; imports, which averaged 109,000 tons in the years 1890-93, reached 1.3 million tons in 1963.

Food imports first became necessary as a result of the

widespread introduction of crops produced specifically
for sale on the world's markets. The great variety and
value of its commercial crops distinguishes Indonesia
among primary producing countries. Products which
are, or have been, major exports include rubber, sugar,
tea, tobacco, coffee, copra, cinchona, cocoa, kapok, palm
oil, pepper, and nutmeg. Many of these are exotic crops
introduced by the European powers—coffee for example
was brought to Java by the Dutch in the 17th century,
while tea, cinchona, rubber, and the oil palm reached
the archipelago in the 19th and 20th centuries. Production is conducted in a variety of ways, but a primary
distinction is that between the peasant producer and the
estates or plantations. The latter have degenerated sadly
from their heyday in the first three decades of this century. The decline began in the great depression of the
inter-war years when primary product (i.e. food and raw
material) prices plunged, and continued during the
Japanese occupation and the subsequent war against the
Dutch. Latterly, the new independent government hastened the process by expelling alien owners and managers in pursuance of anti-imperialist policies, for the
army officers who took over management of the expropriated enterprises generally displayed both incom-
petence and corruption.

The Indonesian people, for their part, were quick to
see the possibilities of producing for the world market.
Indeed from time to time during the colonial period the
estates had to take steps to ward off their competition.
Peasant production accounted for about 10 per cent of
exports at the end of the 19th century, but had risen
to 40 per cent by 1938 and to 62 per cent by 1960. In
certain cultivations, for example pepper, nutmeg, and
kapok, smallholders have always dominated the market;
conversely, plantations predominate today as yesterday
in others, such as sugar and palm oil and palm kernels.

Smallholder commercial enterprise developed mainly in the outer islands and is increasingly concentrated there; Java's overpopulation has entailed intensive land use for subsistence in the peasant sector. Generally speaking, smallholder production of commercial crops is combined with subsistence farming, so that when prices drop below a remunerative level there is something to fall back upon. This flexibility stood the smallholder in good stead during the period of wildly fluctuating prices between the wars when many of the big estates found themselves in serious difficulties. Since independence, smuggling has become a major problem. The government, conscious of the need to raise revenue and to earn foreign exchange, has endeavoured to control production and prices of the more important crops such as rubber. The peasants, on the other hand, have tried to evade control in order to concentrate on finding the crop and the outlet yielding the greatest return. This has meant in practice selling to merchants ready to ignore government regulations and to ship produce illegally to Singapore, Malaya, and the Philippines, where good prices can be obtained, and moreover in hard currencies rather than in the greatly depreciated Indonesian rupiah.

Indonesian agriculture is in a serious condition. Total exports in 1960 were less than a third of those in 1928; the once great staple, sugar, which accounted for a third of all Indonesian exports a century ago, is no longer exported at all. The rubber industry, upon which the government relies very heavily (rubber earns nearly half Indonesia's foreign exchange) is desperately in need of re-planting with new high-yield trees like those to be found in neighbouring Malaysia. This would however demand a colossal investment of capital and labour. In the subsistence sector, Java's problems progressively worsen. Historically, the Javanese people have been,

thanks to the outstanding fertility of their island, im-
mune from serious hunger (except during the height of
the notorious 'Culture System' in the eighteen-forties; it
is curious that the same decade is remembered for hunger in Western Europe as well). But at the end of 1961
and again in 1964 famine conditions were reported in
parts of Java and neighbouring Lombok. To tackle Java's
plight would necessitate determined and expensive
government intervention. But to raise the necessary revenue would require effective control of the outer islands'
earnings, and this would certainly intensify the already
significant resentment felt there against the central government. Once before, in 1958, this resentment blew up
into open revolt in Sumatra and Celebes (Sulawesi), so
as well as a serious economic problem there is a delicate
political problem involved.

Two great natural economic assets of Indonesia, as yet
only partially exploited, are fish and forests. Just as this
region is the world's richest in plant species, so the
waters round and between the islands of the archipelago
harbour more edible species of fish than anywhere else
on earth. With a coast-line of 46,000 kilometres (the
world's equatorial circumference is only 40,000) there
are ample opportunities for off-shore fishing. The out-
board motor has meant an extension in the range of the
Indonesian fisherman, but the fishing industry as a
whole is not yet well enough equipped or organized to
take full advantage of the possibilities. Once again,
Japan points the way. Inland, irrigation systems and
flooded padi fields make ideal habitat for reaping a fish
'harvest', though deliberate fish 'farming' has not yet attained on Java the intensity with which it is practised
in densely populated parts of China and Japan. Fish is
of peculiar importance in Indonesia, as in most rice-
growing countries, because it is far and away the most
important source of non-vegetable protein in a diet other-

wise too heavily dependent upon rice and vegetables. Pork is strictly speaking forbidden to Muslims, which most Indonesians profess to be; sheep are not found in the islands; the cattle are largely work animals; and dairying is uncommon.

The forestry potential may be gauged from the fact that most of Indonesia is still covered with trees. The major part of this is secondary forest (*belukar*), the result of natural reforestation after clearance of primeval forest for *swidden* cultivation. Over 80 per cent of Kalimantan and Irian Barat (West New Guinea) are under forest. Because of the range of altitudes and the topographical variety of the archipelago, there is a wide range of timbers represented, including important teak stands on Java, and rare and valuable species such as Timor's sandalwood. The commercial possibilities are great, especially if carefully planned reforestation was to be undertaken on a national scale.

Although agriculture continues to dominate the economic life of Indonesia (to an extent that has not been true of Britain since the 16th century), it is not the whole story. The Dutch did not, except sporadically in special circumstances (for example during the First World War), actively encourage industry in their colony except to the limited extent found useful or necessary for their own purposes. Indeed the Dutch normally sought actively to discourage and prevent local enterprise. Since independence, there have been efforts to develop and extend the industrial sector, but so far with limited success. Corruption, inexperience, and lack of foreign exchange have resulted in many of the existing plants running well below capacity or even closing down. Most of the enterprises are small—often barely distinguishable from home-based handicraft industries; the majority are to be found in Java; and there is a marked concentration on the processing and production of essential consumer goods such as food and tobacco products and clothing. By 1958 industry contributed only 11 per cent to the gross domestic product of Indonesia; this contrasts with the 50 per cent contribution industry makes on average to the gross domestic products of high-income countries such as those of Western Europe and North America.

In relation to the level of economic development of the country, the extent of urbanization in Indonesia is excessive. In 1930 Indonesia, with a population at that time of 61 million, had only seven cities with 100,000 or more inhabitants, all but one on Java. Today, Indonesia boasts no fewer than 21 cities in the 100,000+ bracket, ten of them in the outer islands, mostly in Sumatra. This rapid build-up of big unplanned conurbations has had disastrous consequences, for people have been flocking in, not in response to job opportunities in the cities, but in reaction to over-crowding and the absence of opportunities in the countryside. Under the strain city amenities, never adequate, have sadly deteriorated. All the characteristic slum problems, brewed from poverty, congestion, infected water, and faulty drainage and sanitation have appeared: infant mortality rates reaching and exceeding 500 per 1,000 (Britain's was 22 per 1,000 in 1964, and Sweden's 15); ubiquity of infectious and contagious diseases; high crime rates; prostitution; and juvenile delinquency. Djakarta, a city of half a million in the thirties, today has over 3 million inhabitants, and the great status-buildings like the Hotel Indonesia tower above a sea of shacks.

The big cities form only one of the urban categories in Indonesia. Clifford Geertz, an American anthropologist, describes a Javanese town of 24,000—typical of a hundred others on Java—as follows: '. . . a banyan tree with a Hindu statue at its foot in the public square; a cluster of government offices centered round the District

Officer's house with its traditional deep veranda and broad front yard; a line of open-fronted, awning-shaded Chinese stores and warehouses; a large, open market place with rusted tin sheds and wooden stalls; a mosque, gleaming a painful white in the tropical sun; and hundreds of small bamboo-walled, dirt-floored houses crowded helter-skelter on to the large blocks formed by the street grid. There are a motion picture theater, two small hospitals, a government pawnshop, a couple of dozen elementary and secondary schools, a bus depot, and a narrow-gauge railway with station, repair shop, and miniature wood-burning locomotives which look like fanciful Victorian toys.' Such a typical Javanese town would be set in a checkered pattern of rice fields.

Even inside Java there are, of course, variations, while in the outer islands there is great diversity in the pattern of towns and provincial cities, from those of Hinduized Bali to the China towns of West Borneo. Village types range from the long-houses of Indonesian Borneo (Kalimantan) to the elaborate and embellished villages of parts of Sumatra and Java.

Transport and communications present serious problems for a country such as Indonesia, sprawling and poor. It is true that this is an archipelago; the sea links island with island and port with port (this is an advantage where transport facilities are scarce and simple; Britain's long coastline has always been recognized to have been an important factor in her early industrialization). On the other hand, the complex of islands and maze of channels also facilitated piracy in the past, and the area harboured such famous pirate peoples as the Bugis and the Makassarese. Moreover, it is one thing to maintain communications by means of thousands of small local craft—praus and junks—quite another to operate large-scale modern shipping lines catering for both freight and passengers in the volume and numbers and with the regularity now called for, as the Indonesians quickly discovered when political differences with the Dutch in the nineteen-fifties led to interruption in the working of the Koninklijke Paketvaart Mij. (KPM) which at one time carried practically all the inter-island traffic.

Inland transport facilities are underdeveloped. This was not always so, for visitors to Java in the 19th century were impressed by the road network and horse-drawn express service constructed and operated by the Netherlands Indies administration. Daendels, who was Governor from 1808 to 1811, drove a magnificent road through from Anjer, the western extremity of the island, to Banjuwangi, the eastern extremity, in less than two years. But his methods involved forced labour and summary hanging for those who failed to complete their allocated quota of road on time. Nevertheless, the road shortened the overland east-west journey at a stroke from forty days to six and a half. Western contemporaries, interestingly enough, did not consider the terrible loss of 'native' life involved reprehensible or regrettable. Construction of railways began in 1864. State and private enterprise shared the task, and both orthodox railways and steam-tramways were laid down. Java by the 20th century had a network comparable with that of European countries in terms of density, but the outer islands were sparsely provided for. Nor were the Dutch slow to see the advantages of another Victorian invention— the electric telegraph. The first British telegraph company was formed in 1846, and the cable did not cross the Atlantic till 1866, nor reach Australia till 1871. Yet W. B. D'Almeida, a visitor to Java in the early eighteen-sixties, noted electric telegraph lines throughout the island.

However, the early and solid start was not consolidated. The tremendous boom in rubber and other primary products came to an end after 1929. Crisis was followed by Japanese invasion and a long struggle with the Dutch for independence. Subsequently, political squabbling diverted attention from reconstruction. The result is that today Indonesia still has fewer miles of railway, fewer locomotives, and less rolling stock than in the nineteen-thirties. The roads have likewise deteriorated. In terms of such indices as surfaced roads per 1,000 inhabitants, or length of railways per 100 square miles, Indonesia emerges in comparison with the countries of the West as badly underdeveloped. The contrast with her developed Asian neighbour Japan is revealing. In 1963 Indonesia had fewer than 100,000 commercial motor vehicles on her roads; Japan, with a slightly smaller population and one-fifth of the area, had nearly 3 million. In 1962 there was roughly one private car for every seven people in Britain; in Indonesia one for every seven hundred. Since then the disparity has appreciably widened.

But cars are luxuries. What is the comparative situation with necessities? There are problems of definition here—what constitutes a 'necessity' is largely a cultural appraisal—but food is indisputably necessary. The figures we have are more or less rough estimates, but certain trends and comparative magnitudes are nonetheless clearly discernible. It has been estimated, for example, that average annual rice consumption per head in Java (including, by convention, the neighbouring island of Madura) was as follows:

1856-70 average	114 kilogrammes	
1881-90 „	105.5	„
1891-1900 „	100.6	„
1936-40 „	89.0	„
1960 „	81.4	„

But rice is not the only foodstuff and this falling off in rice consumption was accompanied by a growing importance of non-rice foodstuffs in the diet, particularly maize, soya beans, peanuts, and cassava. Thus whereas in 1888 two-thirds of the harvested area was under rice, by 1920 it was down to one half of the total, and by 1938 to 45 per cent. It was possible by diversification and rotation to drive the terraces ever harder to keep abreast of rising population. But the result was seriously to lower the adequacy of the diet in many areas. This is reflected in the available figures for calories per head per day: the 1921-25 average was 1,803, while that of 1935-39 was 1,718. The Food and Agriculture Organization of the United Nations calculate that the *minimum* calory requirement for this area—peninsular and insular South-East Asia—is 2,270 per head per day. To give some standard for comparison, average North American daily intake is about 3,110 and average Western European about 3,040. The disparity is much greater when one comes to examine the quality of the calories. For example, whereas North Americans absorb some 66 grammes of animal protein per day, Indonesians have to be satisfied with something like a tenth of that.

There is little doubt that on Java things have deteriorated since the war. This is true too on some of the smaller proximate populated islands such as Lombok and Sumbawa, east of Bali. Towards the end of 1961, for example, it was an exceptionally dry spell that precipitated famine in parts of Java and Lombok. Again, a poor crop in 1965 is said to have resulted in the deaths of between 10,000 and 30,000 people on Lombok between November that year and April 1966. These are sobering occurrences in what has been throughout history a region apparently super-endowed with fertile soils and the capacity to feed whatever additional millions human fertility produced. The future threatens to be darker still. Population projections would suggest a Javanese population of about 150 million by the end of the century—on an area roughly comparable with New York State. Clearly long before that point has been reached either radical change or catastrophe must intervene.

Matters are different in the other islands, where there is cultivable land available. Moreover, smallholder producers of commercial crops can afford to buy imported food with their foreign exchange earnings.

It is one of the hazards of writing about Indonesia that it is difficult to do justice to its diversity. Nearly all generalizations require considerable qualification. It is significant that the national motto is *Bhinneka Tunggal Ika,* meaning 'unity in diversity'. We have already noted more than once the broad division between Java and the other, or outer, islands. But this is by no means the whole story. Inhabiting the Indonesian islands are something like 366 distinct ethnic groups; of these ten to a dozen have over a million members each and their own distinctive language, social pattern, and history.

However, before attempting to sketch the major polarities and distinctions in Indonesian life, it may be useful to draw attention to some of the broad cultural similarities. For example, although over 250 distinct languages are spoken in the archipelago, most belong to one linguistic family—the Malayo-Polynesian, sharing many close cognate words and possessing highly similar grammatical structures. Moreover, the nationalist movement, in one of its shrewdest moves, quite early on decided to promote a national language. This was based on Malay, some knowledge of which was not uncommon among the peoples of the archipelago, particularly those on or near the coast, as a regional commercial *lingua franca*; it was also the cultural language of Islam in the area. The decision to promote a national language —*Bahasa Indonesia*—was taken at an All-Indonesia

Youth Congress in 1928, and thereafter enthusiastically forwarded by Indonesian intellectuals and leaders as an important element in nationalism.

Other common characteristics that may be cited include profession of Islam—by about 95 per cent of the Indonesian population—an underlying general cultural influence of Hinduism and Indian values and patterns, and an even deeper and earlier general, indigenously rooted, animism. Belief in spirits, and in the various modes adopted to influence them, is not thought incompatible with profession of faith in a higher religion such as Islam, Buddhism, or Christianity; this is actually true for South-East Asia as a whole as much as for Indonesia.

There are other rather widely spread common cultural characteristics which Indonesia shares with her neighbours, among which may be mentioned a rather privileged or 'democratic' or emancipated position for women as compared with customary patterns in South Asia and East Asia. In many respects, South-East Asian women have a status and a freedom closer to that found in Europe and North America than to that found in India and in China before the Revolution: they talk freely with strangers, play an important part in planning family budgets and family affairs in general, and undertake many of the marketing and commercial transactions. It is also the case in South-East Asia, including Indonesia, that the small nuclear family of parents and children is the typical unit rather than the large extended family of most of the rest of Asia.

Having said as much, it is time to return to the tremendous cultural diversity to be observed in Indonesia. The overwhelming allegiance to Islam, for instance, conceals important and significant distinctions. In accordance with distinct socio-cultural traditions, observance may be token or it may be strict. The former situation is especially characteristic of the culture associated in origin with the heartland of Java—the central inland valleys known by the Javanese as 'Mataram' after the great historical island kingdom. Here, Hindu influences have remained strong in both aesthetic and religious terms. Once the culture especially of the court and gentry (*prijaji*), this is now the prevailing pattern for white-collar Javanese in general, and is referred to by the term *prijaji*.

On the other hand, Java houses another distinct tradition where observance of Islam is much more orthodox. This originated especially along the north coast, in the ports open to commercial and other influences from outside. It spread from these areas all over the island, but to a large extent retaining its original associations with trade. This tradition has been dubbed *santri* to distinguish it from *prijaji*. The distinction is an extremely important one for an understanding of Indonesian history and politics.

A third Javanese religious tradition, rooted in the peasantry, is that referred to as *abangan*. Nominally Muslim, the practitioners in reality ceremoniously endeavour to placate a variety of spirits including Allah and Muslim religious heroes, but also Hindu gods and indigenous Javanese spirits. The key ritualistic expression here is the *slametan* or ceremonial meal periodically shared by a small group of immediate neighbours, and symbolizing the dominant value of Javanese culture —mutual co-operation or *gotong rojong*.

It should be noted that Java has also two other significant and quite separate ethno-linguistic groups—Madurese in the east and Sundanese in the west, each with distinctive culture patterns. There are also, here as elsewhere in Indonesia, extremely important minority groups, notably the Chinese, but also including Arabs, Indians, and others.

Outside Java, a number of broad cultural distinctions may be made. At the eastern extremity of Indonesia, for example, are to be found Papuans on West Irian (West New Guinea). Moving west, the next-door group of islands, known as the South Moluccas, display certain a-typical characteristics. Many of the inhabitants in fact claim closer relationship with the Melanesians to the east than with the broadly Malay types to the west. The South Moluccas group is also highly Christianized, unlike the rest of Indonesia, and it was from this area that the Dutch recruited for their colonial armies. To be exhaustive, one would certainly also have to discuss separately and in some detail such distinctive groups as the Makassarese; Buginese; Land Dyaks and Ibans of Kalimantan; and the Atjehnese, Minangkabau, and Bataks of Sumatra.

However, there is a recognizably single—if hetero-geneous—culture which embraces the peoples of eastern Sumatra, the islands between Sumatra and Borneo, the coasts and river-valleys of Borneo, and the coastal peoples of Atjeh, South Celebes, and many of the other islands of the eastern part of Indonesia. This has been called 'Pasisir' or coastal culture. It has, historically, roots in the international spice trade, and early adopted and spread Islam. Occupationally, its members typically en-gage in a variety of agricultural and other pursuits, including both wet-rice and *swidden* cultivation, com-mercial farming, inter-island trade, and fishing.

The Minangkabau and Bataks of west Sumatra have a number of interesting distinguishing features. By origin inland and highland peoples, rapid social change in the last hundred years has produced important new variants. The Toba-Bataks have been Christianized. The Minangkabau have shown an aptitude for commerce and business, and have migrated to all parts of Indone-sia in search of profitable openings. Minangkabau society has long been of special interest to anthropologists and sociologists, since it is matrilinear; that is, on marriage the bridegroom joins the bride's family and clan.

It is clear, even from a survey as brief as the foregoing, just how great is the diversity referred to in the Indonesian national motto. Even such an apparently homogeneous minority community as the Chinese—between two and three million of them—is divided into those with very long associations with the archipelago, perhaps going back many generations, and to some extent culturally assimilated, and known as *Peranakan*, and the more recent immigrants, often China-orientated and culturally exclusivist and excluded, known as *Totoks*. The former were drawn largely from the Hokkein, the latter from the Hakkas and Cantonese.

It is understandable, therefore, that the nationalists both before and after independence placed such special emphasis and importance on the task of nation-building. Geographical dispersion; cultural diversity; religious, language, class, and race differences; all these and other potential sources of disintegration in Indonesian society had to be combatted. How successfully national leaders have tackled the urgent problem of national unity subsequent chapters aim to show.

2

THE LEGACY OF THE PAST

THE area now known as Indonesia has been inhabited for a very long time. Remains discovered in Java and attributed to *Pithecanthropus erectus, Homo modjokertensis* and *Homo soloensis* suggest that one of the earliest races of mankind may have originated in the archipelago. There are also traces of an early and distinct culture known as the Veddoid, descendants of whom are still to be found in small backward communities in the south Celebes and on the Engalo and Mentawai Islands off the west coast of Sumatra. But controversy persists about the very earliest period, so slight is the available evidence.

Most present-day Indonesians, are, however, descended from 'Malay' peoples moving southwards into the region between two and three millenia ago from Western China via mainland South-East Asia. Much has been written about outside influences on Indonesia—the successive impacts of Hinduism, Islam, and the Dutch. But there was a recognizable and indigenous local civilization in Indonesia before those forces made themselves felt. This civilization was the achievement of the 'Malay' peoples.

The cultivation of 'wet' (irrigated) rice was already the basis of civilized society in the Indonesian islands at this early stage—historically pre-dating the advent of civilization to Britain. (A society may be said to have achieved civilization at that point in its development when settled agriculture has become proficient enough in food production to permit some division of labour, a part of the population becoming specialists in some non-agricultural pursuit—metallurgy, religion, warfare, and commerce, for example.) Ox and buffalo were domesticated, and metals such as gold, copper, iron, and bronze were worked. As befitted the inhabitants of an island complex, the Indonesians understood the principles of seamanship and navigation sufficiently well to allow them latterly to undertake long ocean voyages, to China in the east and to Ceylon and India in the west (and possibly to Madagascar and East Africa as well).

The prevalent religion was animist—that is to say the people attributed living souls, motives, and agency to inanimate objects and natural phenomena. Ancestors were worshipped, and burial procedures were elaborate. The prevailing world-view or philosophy appears to have been based upon an apprehension of the duality of nature—the contradiction of opposites such as mountain and sea, winged beings and water beings, hill people and plains people.

It appears that a number of characteristically Indonesian artistic accomplishments were already in evidence, including *wajang* (a puppet theatre in which the audience watches the shadows of the manipulated wood and leather figures thrown on a screen by appropriately placed lights), *gamelan* (an orchestra of complex instrumentation producing highly intricate music which has been described as '. . . comparable only to two things: moonlight and running water. It is pure and mysterious like moonlight, it is always the same and always changing like flowing water'), and production of *batik* (the subtly patterned wax-resist dyed cloth). All have persisted to this day with great vigour; there were more than 17,000 *gamelan* in Java, for example, just before the Second World War. The strength of indigenous tradition is also attested by the continuing vitality of the original *gamelan* instrumentation. Indian-influenced instruments apparently appeared and disappeared in the past, but the ancient Indonesian instruments survive, however modified by time. As far as literature is concerned, a 10th-century Javanese version of the Indian

29

Ramayana is said to show 'such an accomplishment of style and mastery of form that it must be the product of a far older literary tradition', while evidence points to an ancient Malay literary tradition as well. Throughout recorded history, then, music, dance, and verse have been important motifs in Indonesian culture.

Another major motif has been the evolution of patterns of social behaviour making for tranquil personal relationships and for the minimum of conflict. It is not hard to establish the reasons for this. Wet rice cultivation demands irrigation, and irrigation demands social co-operation. The water must be regulated and allocated. If this is not done amicably the livelihood of the village may be threatened. Moreover, the rice crop periodically demands concentrated attention. This is true when the seedlings are being transplanted in the prepared field, for example, and at harvest time. At these times the help of neighbours is vital. In such circumstances reciprocity is a practical necessity in addition to whatever claims it may have to being a moral imperative. The system of land tenure strengthened the natural demands of rice itself. Individual and family rights to occupy, work, and bequeath land were respected, much as if the plots were privately owned. But in practice the community as a whole reserved ultimate responsibility. From the early centuries, when specifically Indonesian civilization was first becoming established, the social outlook of *gotong rojong*, mutual co-operation (*rukun* in Javanese), has persisted as an underlying and idiosyncratic constant of Indonesian society and history.

The existence of the Indonesian archipelago may have been known to the Alexandrine geographer Ptolemy, and the Indian text *Vayu Purana* mentions *Malayadvipa* (Sumatra) and *Yavadvipa* (Java and Sumatra). Chinese records early acknowledge the existence of Java (*Ye-p'o-ti*) and of an important commercial centre in the south-east of Sumatra (*Ko-ying*). These references date from the early centuries A.D.

Rivalry between Java and Sumatra is an important recurring theme of Indonesian history which has persisted to the present day. In terms of historical geography the reason was that the shortest sea route between the East and the West passes through the Malacca strait, which divides Sumatra from Malaya. Settlements on the shores of this narrow length of water have as a result an outstanding natural advantage. Sumatra clearly dominates the strait, a circumstance favourable alike to extraction of dues from passing shipping and to piracy, both lucrative pursuits. But there is an alternative route through this crossroad of international commerce—the Sunda strait, which divides Java and Sumatra. The Sunda passage always threatened, therefore, to break Sumatra's monopoly of control over international shipping. Moreover, Java had two important counter-advantages in their rivalry. The first was a more central position in the archipelago. This was important in facilitating access to and control of valuable products in the islands east of Sumatra (for example, the spices of the Moluccas). The second was more fertile and varied soil. The importance of this was in turn two-fold: in enabling Java to support a higher population than her neighbour, and in making possible the production of a variety of commercially acceptable commodities for export. (Though in the 5th and 6th centuries A.D. we hear of Sumatran pine resin, benzoin, and camphor entering international commerce.)

Superimposed upon this pattern came the layers of powerful external influences which were successively to leave permanent impressions on Indonesian society and history. The first of these, chronologically, was the influence of India. From the first century A.D. onwards Indian visitors to Indonesia, and—just as important—

Indonesian visitors to India returning home, were introducing Indian ideas to the archipelago. This is reflected
in Indonesian architecture, dancing, *wajang* stories, and
countless other respects. But we may discuss this period
of paramount Indian impact, which lasted over one
thousand years, predominantly in terms of Hinduism
and Buddhism.

There had been small political units in Indonesia before the advent of the Indian-influenced kingdoms
(generally known by the term 'Hindu-Javanese'), but
they lacked the organization, cohesion, and endurance
which the Indian example, copied and applied, could
supply. The principle elements of this example were
these: attribution of divinity to kings ('god-kings'); the
use of the classical Sanskrit language; promulgation of
Indian mythology as embodied in such texts as the
Ramayana and *Mahabharata*; and observance of the
Dharmasastra (the sacred law of Hinduism). The principal mode of transmission of this influence was probably the appearance at Indonesian courts of Brahmins,
whose position at Indian courts had become familiar
to Indonesian traders to India. Brahmins were members
of the Hindu priestly caste, and it was their function to
consecrate god-kings in accordance with classical Indian
usages. That Indian merchants alone could not have
exerted the critical cultural influence is suggested by
the failure of Chinese merchants—who also visited the

---

1. *Indonesian faces*
   (a) A typical Indonesian in the characteristic black velvet cap
       (*pitji*).
   (b) A stallholder in the public market in Makassar, Sulawesi
       (Celebes).
   (c) A young woman from Kalimantan (Indonesian Borneo) wear-
       ing traditional costume embroidered with gold and silver
       thread.
   (d) A young woman from West Java. Her umbrella is an ex-
       ample of local handicrafts.

archipelago—to impart to Indonesian society an equivalent element of the equally ancient and sophisticated Chinese culture.

Buddhism, too, was conveyed to Indonesia in the early centuries of the Christian era. Missionaries from India visited Indonesian courts and established monasteries, while Indonesian converts in turn went to study in India. But Buddhism in Indonesia tended to go hand in hand with other elements. Buddhist courts, for example, would still employ Brahmins. This illustrates a characteristic aspect of Indonesian history—the ability to effect a synthesis of different ingredients, accepting the new without discarding the old, absorbing and blending rather than substituting. Moreover, it is important to bear in mind that the influence of both Buddhism and Hinduism was first and foremost felt at court; for the mass of the people the indigenous culture remained primary, although in time, and unevenly, both Hinduism and Buddhism had their effect even at the popular level, percolating outwards and downwards socially from the aristocracy, filtered bit by bit for relevant and acceptable components that could readily be accommodated by, and incorporated into, the existing peasant cultural and value system. Plays based on Indian epic themes, for example, became the staples of Indonesian *wajang*. *Batik* designers borrowed Indian motifs. Javanese and Balinese dance took much from India too. Of the Hindu gods, Siva or Shiva (lord of the cosmic dance of creation and destruction, and associated with fertility) was made particularly welcome in the Indonesian pantheon. The deepest and most lasting impact of Hinduism was felt in the island of Bali. On the other hand, the Hindu caste system in its full rigour had little

---

2. *Indonesian villages*
   (*a*) A village in Java.
   (*b*) A village in Sumatra.

appeal in Indonesia. Nor did Indian influence affect the position of women in Indonesian society.

Our knowledge of the many states which rose, flourished, and collapsed during this period is tantalizingly incomplete—indeed fragmentary. But there were those among them that extended further, endured longer, and achieved more than their contemporaries. Of these, two stand out—Srivijaya and Madjapahit (there are several alternative transliterations for the names of these two powers—for example Sriwidjaja and Modjapait). Each at its peak, in the 9th and 14th centuries respectively, appears to have dominated an area roughly co-extensive with the area later administered by the Netherlands East Indies and its successor the Republic of Indonesia, with, in addition, colonies elsewhere in South-East Asia.

Srivijaya was a Sumatra-based, Buddhist, and maritime-commercial power. Waxing and waning, it lasted from the 7th to the 13th centuries. Unlike its contemporary rivals on Java, Srivijaya, for all its accomplishments, left little in the way of permanent architectural monuments to its greatness. But at its height it played an important role in international trade, handling such articles as ivory, sugar, dates, preserved peaches, rhinoceros horn, perfumes, spices, glass bottles, cotton cloth, and naptha. Its capital city was in the vicinity of present-day Palembang. Srivijaya was renowned as a centre of Buddhist learning, and attracted scholars from all over the East. Conversely, mercenary soldiers from this great state are said to have served as far afield as West Asia ('the Middle East').

During this period, the kingdoms of Java were in general too divided successfully to challenge the Sumatran power for long, but the Shailendra dynasty and the successor state, Mataram, based on Central and East Java, did so for a time in the 8th, 9th, and 10th centuries. These Hindu-Javanese kingdoms were also influenced by Buddhism, but less pervasively than Srivijaya. These were also, in contrast, most typically land-based agricultural powers, ruled by god-kings and their bureaucracies. Among their lasting achievements are superb architectural monuments, best known of which is Borobudur, near Jogjakarta. This is a Buddhist *stupa* (reliquary mound) built in the 8th century around the summit of a hill, and rising in nine stages to a crowning pinnacle. The galleries round the terraces are over three miles in length all told, and there are thousands of sculptures depicting Buddha's life. The monument celebrates both the Buddhist stages to individual salvation and the cosmos itself.

The empire of Madjapahit was founded in 1293, the year following the visit of the first European to reach Indonesia—Marco Polo. It is remembered chiefly now for the achievements of its prime minister Gadjah Mada, who ruled from 1331 to 1364. He succeeded in re-uniting the archipelago, codifying local law and custom, standardizing administration, and improving the revenue system. Art and literature flourished, contacts were made with neighbouring Asian powers, and both Buddhism and Hinduism were accepted. Despite its great achievements, Madjapahit's empire lasted less than a century, though a kingdom of that name lingered on into the 16th century, when it finally disintegrated under a number of pressures, of which the chief was Islam. Later still, Sultan Agung, who ruled Mataram from 1613 to 1645, invoked the glories of Madjapahit in extending his sway over much of Java and parts of the outer islands.

But before turning to consider the impact of Islam, reference ought to be made to the position of the Chinese in the area at this time, for at a later date the Chinese were to constitute a significant portion of the Indonesian population. China had had trade and court-level contacts with South-East Asia from the earliest times of which we have substantial record. But permanent Chinese settlers remained sparse until Western rule, with its protection, was confirmed in the region. In the pre-colonial period there were Chinese merchants in the principal seaports, and a handful of others scattered elsewhere as chance or mischance took them. The big immigrations were still in the future.

The reasons for the decline of Madjapahit and the spread of Islam were closely related. We have seen how important international trade was for the Indonesian islands. Even those kingdoms based on control of agricultural wealth in Java invariably extended their activities into regional control of trade during periods of ascendancy. This was true of Madjapahit, whose ports on the north coast of Java were obviously advantageously placed to intervene in East-West traffic—for example passing the much-prized spices of the Moluccas (in eastern Indonesia) on to India and ultimately to the Mediterranean through West Asia, and in return distributing the products of West and South Asia back through the Indonesian islands and on to East Asia.

This chain of commerce was naturally accompanied by two-way human contact, and among those visiting South-East Asia from early times for purposes of trade were Arabs. The rapid expansion of Islam in the Arab world after its birth in the 7th century inevitably had eventual repercussions all along the linked eastern trade routes. Arab merchants brought word of the new doctrines to the ports with which they traded. An important impetus to the spread of Islam in Indonesia and Malaysia came from the conversion of Gujerat, on India's north-west coast, because Gujerati merchants were active in maritime South-East Asia. Marco Polo found a Muslim principality in northern Sumatra in the late 13th century. But the turning point was to come with the rise at Malacca, on Malaya's south-west coast, of a successful commercial entrepôt, under able administrators of the Muslim faith, in the early 15th century. Muslim merchants of many nations chose to centre their dealings on Malacca, and the commercial strings of the region tended by a natural process increasingly to tie up there. Back along the resulting network ran the impulses of Islam, to captivate ruler after ruler of the coastal cities of the archipelago—in Sumatra, in northern Java, and eastwards to Celebes and the Moluccas.

At first, the inland-based Javanese kingdoms resisted in the name of their deep-rooted religious traditions. But as their power flagged before the steadily recruited Islamic enemy, even these Hindu heartlands, in self-defence, embraced the new faith—at least in name and form. The island of Bali alone defied the tide of Islam to keep alive the old glories of Hindu-Javanese culture. In Java the peasant generally seems to have made way readily enough in his existing spirit-god world for the new Deity, and gradually adjusted his behaviour patterns to the new observances without jettisoning the tried and familiar. This kind of adaptation by synthesis contrasted somewhat with the earlier and more spontaneous conversions obtaining in the north coast towns of Java and parts of Sumatra, especially among those associated with commerce and trade. The contrast was to supply a persistent cross-current in all subsequent Indonesian history.

The acceptability of Islam to Indonesians was much enhanced by being conveyed to them after the beginning of the 13th century predominantly in the *Sufi* form. *Sufi* mysticism accorded much more closely with the mysticism which had underlain all previous Indonesian religions than did Islam in its more scholastic forms. *Sufi* mystics apparently travelled with visiting merchants from West and South Asia, to settle in Indonesia. On arrival they generally kept up their associations with the business community. At court level they were accepted as dispensers of legitimacy, much as the Brahmins had been before them, transforming in this instance rajahs into sultans.

In assessing the long-term consequences for Indonesia of the coming of Islam it is suggestive to recall the more or less simultaneous impact of Islam on Western Europe. Western Europe in its dark ages had almost entirely lost touch with the root Judaeo-Greek tradition, sunk instead as it was in empty religious formalism, obscurantism and worse. Contact with Islam revived in the West acquaintance with and appreciation of scientific method, and gave access to important inventions and major scholarly works, some old and long lost to the West, others new. The result was the laying of the foundations for Western intellectual revival and scientific achievement, with consequences that were ultimately to transform the world.

But in South-East Asia, too, Islam paved the way for more modern world-views. In doing so, it pioneered 'modernization' in the region *before* the advent of the Europeans. In Indonesia the spread of Islam laid the foundations for the acceptance of Malay as the national language, to take one example. Malay was the *lingua franca* of traders in the region, and it was this social group that first embraced Islam. Malay in fact became one of the major languages of Muslim culture, the vehicle for religious and philosophical literature as well as for history and popular romances. Its use spread, with Islam, through the archipelago.

Because its adherents believed that there was but one God, Islam also undermined the traditional oligarchic, rigid and hierarchical social systems under a god-king. Other Islamic ideas were potentially democratic; at a later date socialist theories were to reach Indonesia from two sources—European Marxism and Middle Eastern Islamic reformism.

There are other interesting aspects of this. Europe's expansion was made *possible* by her intellectual revival, to which contact with Islam had contributed; it was made *necessary* by the interference of Islamic powers with great traditional trade routes between the Mediterranean and the West on the one hand and India and the East on the other. The feud of Christianity and Islam in the Western world was thereupon exported half way round the globe to South-East Asia, where the arrival of the first Europeans seeking trade in the 16th century undoubtedly accelerated the conversion of Indonesia to Islam in a 'nationalistic' reaction. Later in Indonesian history, Islam was to provide a most important symbol and rallying point for the genuinely modern nationalist movement.

Initially the arrival of Europeans did not significantly alter the Indonesian scene. Later this was to change. But one of the major mistakes of history written in the West during the colonial period was to suggest that once the colonial powers had arrived autonomous local history ceased. This was of course very far from the truth. The early Portuguese, Spaniards, Dutchmen, and others had at first to fit into a long-established pattern of commerce. Local emporia were the equal of anything Europe had then to offer: indeed Malacca was at that time regarded by Western visitors as the greatest port for international commerce in the world, clearing annually more shipping than any other. As far as technological, navigational, and other accomplishments of a similar kind were concerned, the decisive gap which was (in time) to give the West the edge had not yet opened up.

Nevertheless, the Portuguese took Malacca in 1511, and in 1522 gained direct access to the Moluccas or

Spice Islands by obtaining leave to build a fort in Tern-
ate. A year before, in 1521, the Spanish had established
a settlement in neighbouring Tidore. Simultaneously,
however, Muslim power was increasing steadily in the
archipelago, and if the Portuguese controlled the Malacca Straits, the Muslim merchants controlled the
Sunda Straits. Reaction to the harshness of Portuguese
rule in those areas affected by it was, moreover, strong,
and at the end of the 16th century the future fate of
the archipelago was by no means clear. But the power of
Portugal and Spain was obviously on the wane. Permanent traces of their influence remain in the form of small
pockets of Catholicism, for unlike the later Protestant
powers, they were keen proselytizers, and also in the
valuable new crops introduced by them to the area
from Latin America.

The British cast covetous eyes on the region for a
time—Francis Drake sailed through the archipelago in
1579 and Cavendish in 1586, while shortly after its incorporation in 1600 the English East India Company set
up a 'factory' (trading post) at Bantam on the western
tip of Java in 1602. But it was the Dutch who finally
emerged as the chief external contenders for power in
Indonesia. Following the example of the British, they
formed the Netherlands' United East India Company
(V.O.C.) in 1602. This succeeded in concentrating Dutch
energies in the area, and in time was to exclude all
European rivals from the trade of the Indonesian
islands.

In practice the Company adapted its activities at first
very largely to the existing trade patterns, as other
traders had done before. A Dutch historian comments:
'It carried on trade at the many trading points every-
where in the archipelago in the same way as Oriental
traders and on the same footing, buying cloves on
Ambon from the Ambonese *orang kaya* [nobleman] in

his house, on the scales of the nobleman, as the Javanese trader did; buying pepper in Jambi alongside the Chinese small engrossers from men come down from Minangkabau, buying on no larger a scale than the Jambi court lords and the Javanese, Malay, and Chinese traders coming there. In Achin [Atjeh] it was subjected to the imposition of a toll by the *panglima* [commander] just the same as everyone else.'

The Company was anxious at first to avoid the responsibilities and costs of territorial governance, except to the extent warranted by the need to secure its factories in Java, the Moluccas, and Celebes. Indeed with the other powers in the region in the 17th and 18th centuries—Makassar on the south-west coast of Celebes, Atjeh in Sumatra, Bantam and Mataram in Java, for example—Holland's relations were really in their essential character *international* relations. In time the Company was drawn inexorably into assuming territory and, with it, responsibility. This followed naturally from entanglement in clashes between local principalities and in succession disputes. Nevertheless, it is really misleading to speak of Indonesia as a Dutch *colony* until the last quarter of the 19th century.

It is not possible adequately to summarize the complex pattern of Indonesian history in the two centuries before 1800. All that can be attempted here is to indicate some significant features.

The first priority of the Company was to achieve and enforce a monopoly of trade against the other European powers with an interest in the region—principally Britain, France, Portugal, Spain, and Denmark. This had been substantially accomplished by 1641, the year in which Malacca fell to the Dutch (though Britain retained some factories in Sumatra until 1824, and the Portuguese to this day occupy the eastern half of the island of Timor). Henceforward the ships of alien powers poached in the ports of the archipelago at their peril.

The next, and complementary, task was to ensure exclusive access to the commercially exploitable wealth of Indonesia. To begin with, the Dutch concentrated on the spices—the cloves and the nutmeg and the pepper —which for so long had lured the merchants of the world. But exclusive access alone was not enough for the rapacious Dutch Company and its venal servants: the people of Banda and the other islands of the Moluccas were mercilessly massacred, enslaved, and beggared in pursuit of maximum profit. Nor were the people elsewhere to be spared Dutch exactions. The Company, despite its coastal posts there, had originally underestimated the economic potential of Java. But in the course of the 18th century a new and ultimately even more lucrative source of revenue was opened—forced deliveries (later these were to be the key feature of the notorious *Cultuurstelsel* or Culture System). In the Preanger district of West Java, south of Batavia, the peasants were compelled to cultivate coffee—a crop new to the archipelago and introduced by the Dutch—and to deliver it up to the Company for exportation and sale.

Having established their capital at Batavia, the Dutch found themselves forced to expand in the process of protecting their enclaves, subduing defiant local rulers, and supporting pliant claimants. By the end of the 17th century the Company had acquired the western third of Java; by the end of the 18th century it had added the eastern tip of the island and a belt along the northern coast. Moreover, although five small 'independent' Javanese states survived (including Jogjakarta and Surakarta—successor states of Mataram), they were in practice vassals of the Company, and Dutch residents 'advised' their rulers. Outside Java, rulers who threatened the Company's monopoly were one by one reduced to vassalage (though Borneo and Sumatra largely evaded the Company's power and Atjeh remained independent from the Dutch until the beginning of the present century).

During the course of the 18th century the Company's economic fortunes declined. Corrupt officials milked and mulcted it. A Junior Merchant would pay 3,500 guilders (a guilder was equivalent to 1/8 sterling at gold par) to the Appointments Board for a post carrying a salary of 40 guilders a month, and in practice make 40,000 guilders a year. Furthermore, the importance and profitability of the spice trade of the archipelago declined, factors on both the supply and demand sides militating against the Dutch. Again, the practice of farming out Javanese land and villages to the Chinese for cash was short-sighted and in the end self-defeating, since the exactions of the Chinese impoverished the people. Finally, pirates took a heavy toll of Dutch trade and shipping; there was a nice irony in this since these pirates were commonly Indonesians put out of legitimate business by enforcement of the Dutch monopoly. The Company's bankruptcy was apparent by 1780, and its Charter expired, unmourned and unsung, on 31 December 1799.

There followed a period of some confusion, for although the Netherlands government took over responsibility for the archipelago, there was no coherent policy or plan for its administration and exploitation. Moreover, events elsewhere in the world interfered with the transition from Company to official Dutch rule. During this period, three names stand out—Herman Willem Daendels (Governor-General, 1808-11), Thomas Stamford Raffles (Lieutenant-Governor of the islands on behalf of the English East India Company, 1811-15), and Prince Diponegoro (leader of the nationalist uprising, 1825-30).

Daendels was an administrator of drive and zeal. An English admirer described how he ' . . . proceeded at once to correct abuses in the old Oriental fashion, hanging peculators, European as well as Native, over their own doors without trial. He must have been a man of great energy and intellectual capacity. To him Java owes the admirable system of roads made all over the island in two years, by forced labour, at a great sacrifice of life.' While Governor-General he implemented many reforms, overhauling the machinery of justice, regularizing the administration by converting Javanese hereditary district rulers into civil officials, and selling land (which he declared the property of the sovereign—that is, Holland) to European planters. Daendels believed that private enterprise could extract greater economic benefit for the Netherlands from its colony than could a monopoly such as the Company or some form of state enterprise. He had been influenced by French thinking and experience, and was a 'liberal' in this respect. But there was clear evidence that, in the circumstances of Java, foreign private enterprise unrestrained by any consideration for the local people or by any form of state restriction on its operations, would rapidly have reduced the Javanese to absolute misery and enslavement.

Indonesia fell under British control in 1811 as an incident in the Napoleonic Wars. Authority was exercised by Raffles, another enterprising and energetic administrator (but in addition also a serious student of the history, culture, and language of the region). Like Daendels, he was a 'liberal'—that is, he believed more wealth could be squeezed from the Indonesian islands and people by *laissez faire* than by an inefficient and probably corrupt officialdom. He continued the work of his famous Dutch predecessor by replacing, where possible, indirect rule through the local aristocracy by direct rule from Batavia through provincial administrators. He introduced money taxes in place of forced deliveries, and sold land to European and Chinese capitalists. The theory was that by creating 'money hunger' among the people, who now needed cash to pay taxes (and to buy the imported manufactured products of English industry), they would be forced into earning it by growing commercial crops and/or by working for foreign concerns for wages. In practice, money hunger was usually met by borrowing cash from Chinese or other alien or local money-lenders at crippling rates of interest, while foreign planters and landlords satisfied their labour requirements by feudal exactions of unpaid forced labour.

In 1816 Indonesia was returned to the Dutch and three years later Raffles established Singapore. In 1824 the British and Dutch agreed on a division of 'spheres of influence' in South-East Asia which ended the British presence at Bencoolen in Sumatra and foreshadowed the present boundaries between Malaysia and Indonesia.

At first the Dutch administrators who took over from Raffles were torn between continuing with his principles and reverting to more traditional Dutch methods, based upon delivery of products to them for shipment to and sale in Europe. Finally it was decided to adopt a highly organized form of the latter, known as the Culture System. But before discussing this, it is necessary to glance at Diponegoro's revolt (often referred to as 'the Java War').

There had been revolts against the Dutch before, for example from 1816 to 1818 in the Moluccas under the leadership of Thomas Matulessy, but this one was of more serious dimensions. Enraged by the impoverishment of his people at the hands of foreigners and by inappropriate and insensitive Dutch policies that threatened to ruin the nobility as well, Prince Diponegoro, elder son of the Sultan of Jogjakarta, rose in revolt and launched guerrilla war against the Dutch. From 1825 to 1830 8,000 Europeans lost their lives and 200,000 Javanese, mostly from disease and starvation, since 'burnt earth' tactics were employed on both sides. Eventually the Prince fell into Dutch hands by their treachery and was exiled. Of the Javanese, Raffles had written in his renowned *History of Java* that '. . . ever since the arrival of the Europeans, they have neglected no opportunity of attempting to regain their independence. A reference to the chapters on history will be sufficient to illustrate this, as well as to show the national feeling on the encroachments and assumptions of their European rulers. In the great cause of national independence all would unite . . .' But in this case it was not to be, and the Javanese had to wait nearly another 120 years for political independence.

The long-drawn out war on Java had seriously depleted the Netherlands coffers, and there followed war with Belgium, which after a long struggle succeeded in asserting its independence from Holland. It became, therefore, urgently necessary to find means of making Indonesia pay. The task was entrusted to Van den Bosch, who became Governor-General in 1830. His panacea was the *Cultuurstelsel*.

The Culture System, or system of forced cultivation, was in essence a return to the Preanger system, whereby coffee had been produced for the Company's profit, but with a wider extension of the principle, both in terms of geography and in terms of the range of products embraced, and its more systematic application. In brief, peasants were compelled to grow commercial crops on part of their lands, or to devote part of their labour to the cultivation of government crops grown on wastelands. The two great staples of the system were sugar, an example of a crop grown on peasant land, and coffee, an example of a crop grown on wasteland; between them they accounted for 70 per cent of Indonesian exports at this time and together earned about 97 per cent of the estimated profits of the Culture System.

In theory, the peasant who opted to cultivate commercial crops for the government should have been excused payment of land tax, and should have been paid for his efforts. There were other safeguards written in to the regulations. But in practice all safeguards tended to be swept away and ignored under pressure of Dutch financial needs and the greed of her local agents in Indonesia. Supervisors of the system, both indigenous and Dutch, were rewarded with 'percentages' of the proceeds of the cultivations in the areas for which they were responsible, an arrangement which understandably sharpened their zeal in collection. Demands on the peasantry for forced labour in the fields, in the processing factories, and in the transport and delivery of the produce, passed all reasonable levels. So little time was left to the Javanese for the cultivation of food crops that serious famines occurred in the eighteen-forties. The fertile island had been transformed into a vast Dutch plantation, or, from the point of view of the people, a forced labour camp.

The results of the system were far-reaching. At first glance, it would appear to have been an outstanding success. The total value of exports from Indonesia rose from 12.8 million guilders in 1830 to 74 million guilders in 1840, while the quantity of coffee produced multiplied fourfold, and that of sugar tenfold, during the same period. The Netherlands Trading Company (Nederlandsche Handelmaatschappij—N.H.M.), founded at the instigation of, and partly financed by, the Dutch King in 1825, handled two-thirds of the exports of Java by 1840, and imported cloth and luxury articles for the Javanese and foreigners respectively, thus reviving the Dutch merchant marine and greatly diminishing the

British share in Indonesia's trade, a share which had flourished in the first three decades of the century. At home in the Netherlands, one-third of the budget was derived from the East Indies or India (as Indonesia was called), and this major contribution was used to reduce the national debt, lighten the burden of taxation, build up the Dutch State Railways, and in general improve Holland's social capital. A major cotton industry was founded in the northern provinces of the Netherlands at Twenthe to produce textiles for the Indonesian market.

On the other hand, much of the early success of the system was due to rising prices of coffee and sugar—a fortuitous circumstance unconnected with its merits. Moreover, six of the eight new crops introduced by the government during this period had to be dropped as unprofitable within a short time—even when private planters elsewhere were making a success of them. Forced labour supervised by bureaucrats was not in the long run viable in competition with planters who knew something about the requirements of the respective crops, and various measures had to be taken by the East Indies administrations of the period to discourage private planters and to deprive them of labour. Nor was the influence of the N.H.M. really healthy, for its privileged position made it disinclined to modernize its fleet, and it became side-tracked from its original purposes into acting as banker for the government, with consequences reminiscent of the days of the Company.

For Indonesian society and economy the Culture System marked a serious intensification of colonial intrusion and exploitation. The privileges of the traditional indigenous ruling groups (the *prijaji*), which had been to some extent circumscribed by Daendels and Raffles, were restored by Van den Bosch, who also gave them hereditary succession in office. Under the Culture

System, the *prijaji* had to ensure that the peasants grew what they were required to, and that their labour was available whenever needed. In this, they were closely supervised by Dutch officials. An historian has commented that '. . . this attachment of the *prijaji* to the Dutch administrative hierarchy led to their decline in the eyes of the Indonesians they ruled, detaching them from their traditional social base of support. The lessening prestige was a long-term process, however, and not until the 20th century was their position of leadership seriously threatened by other social groups.' Village headmen, too, were increasingly integrated into the administration at the expense of village harmony and solidarity.

The economic consequences were also serious. In 1830 there was nothing in the comparative circumstances of Java and Japan that would have enabled an economist of the time to predict which of the two was about to embark upon a process of economic development leading to industrialization and modernization. The Culture System meant that the potential investable surplus was siphoned out of Java: in the words of an American anthropologist and student of Indonesia '. . . colonial government was decisive because it meant that the growth potential inherent in the traditional Javanese economy—"the excess labor on the land and the reserves of productivity in the land," to use a phrase which has been applied to the "slack" in the Japanese traditional economy at the Restoration (i.e. the Meiji Restoration of 1868)—was harnessed not to Javanese (or Indonesian) development but to Dutch.' The sweat and toil of the Javanese peasant made possible economic development—in Holland; that of the Japanese peasant made possible the development of an autonomous indigenous industrial sector, which in turn brought immense benefits to the rural sector (in the shape of fertiliser, improved tools, etc). The anthropologist cited above concludes that: 'The real tragedy of colonial history in Java after 1830 is not that the peasantry suffered. It suffered much worse elsewhere, and, if one surveys the miseries of the submerged classes of the 19th century generally, it may even have gotten off relatively lightly. The tragedy is that it suffered for nothing.'

In the peasant sector in Java, the Culture System accelerated a process which was less *evolution* than *involution*. A rapidly growing number of people (and the population of Java more than doubled—from 6 million to 12.7 million—between 1830 and 1860) had to work a much less rapidly expanding area of suitable land by largely traditional methods, more intensively applied.

Finally, the deepening economic penetration set afoot by the system of forced cultivations hastened the destruction of Java's indigenous commercial and industrial sectors. Centuries before, at the zenith of Madjapahit's power, the Javanese economy had been promisingly diversified, with, in addition to agriculture, a wide range of specialized activities, including shipbuilding, iron-working, the founding of brass and copper cannon, and all kinds of trade and commerce. Dutch policy had from the outset interfered with and impeded these non-agricultural pursuits, and the Culture System greatly intensified the process. Imported English and Dutch cotton goods replaced those woven in Java, thus depriving local weavers of their livelihood. In addition, cotton and indigo crops grown for the Javanese textile industry lost their economic purpose. Peasant handicrafts declined, producing rural un- and under-employment. Seafaring men and merchants took to piracy. Internal trade in the new manufactured imports fell largely into the hands of the Chinese and other alien groups, who accordingly flocked into the archipelago at this time.

Cultivation of coffee on behalf of the government lingered on until the First World War, but the Culture System had long before that been replaced. Dissatisfaction with forced cultivation began to make itself apparent both in Holland and the Indies after 1840. There were several reasons for this. First, in the 'forties sugar and coffee prices were less favourable than they had been in the 'thirties, and in consequence the proceeds of the system sagged. Second, and paradoxically, when primary product prices recovered in the 'fifties, it simply served to convince would-be private planters in Holland that they could exploit the wealth of the archipelago more effectively than the government. Chinese and European sub-contractors (for example in the sugar-processing factories) had made vast personal fortunes under the Culture System, and so had those private planters who had succeeded in penetrating the islands in spite of it. By the eighteen-sixties planters were demonstrating conclusively that even crops, such as tobacco, with which forced cultivation methods had failed dismally, could be grown profitably.

Third, the political climate in Holland increasingly favoured the change towards 'liberalism'. This did not imply any growing concern for the peoples of Indonesia; far from it, for both parties subscribed to the view that 'every colony does or ought to exist for the benefit of the mother-country'. However, the wave of bourgeois revolutions which swept Europe in 1848 put the Liberals in power in the Netherlands, and gave the States-General (parliament) for the first time a say in colonial affairs, once the preserve of the monarchy. There followed a series of reforms.

A new constitution for the Netherlands East Indies was enacted in 1854, embodying a number of major changes. But two important matters were not satisfactorily dealt with. The first was control over colonial finance, and the second was the terms upon which private enterprise was to gain access to the wealth of the colony. The former was finally settled in 1864; an Act of that year gave the States-General the power annually to vote the colonial budget. The latter took rather longer.

An early attempt at facilitating the entry of private foreign capital to Indonesia was made in the Act of 1856. But there were two major drawbacks from the point of view of the intending investor—the absence of any provision for heritable leases, and the shortness of permitted leases (twenty years). Nevertheless, stimulated by rising primary product prices on world markets, there was some development of private production as a result. At the same time, the state ceased to cultivate pepper in 1862, cloves and nutmegs in 1863, indigo, tea, cinnamon, and cochineal in 1865, and tobacco in 1866.

The process of 'liberalization' was greatly accelerated in the years around 1870, years which saw improved communications with Europe culminating in the opening of the Suez Canal in 1869 (it was 12,000 miles from London to Singapore via the Cape of Good Hope, 8,000 via the Suez Canal); the rapid expansion of steam shipping at the expense of sail; the development of postal, rail, and telegraph communications inside the Indies, and in the case of the mail and the cable, of links with the rest of the world; and, as further incentive, the continued rise of world primary product prices.

The response in Holland was to pass a series of laws freeing trade and, in general, throwing Indonesia open to private capital. The key measures were both passed in 1870. These were the Agrarian Law and the Sugar Law. The first provided for heritable leases of up to 75 years duration and for the hiring of land from Indonesians. The latter provision was necessary to give sugar companies access to the irrigated fields normally used for wet rice cultivation (sugar thriving in conditions similar to those demanded by rice), without depriving the Indonesians of their livelihood. Indeed, the Law explicitly prohibited the alienation of 'native' land to non-Indonesians. The Agrarian Law, therefore, ostensibly safeguarded Indonesian interests as well, though, as we will see, such safeguards were quite inadequate, and ruthless exploitation of the peoples of the archipelago went on.

The Sugar Law provided for the gradual relinquishment of government cultivation of sugar in twelve annual instalments beginning from 1878. By the end of the century, all the sugar and two-thirds of the coffee in Indonesia were being grown on private account. But the Culture System really died in 1870, and a new era was inaugurated—the era of the great private corporations.

The achievements of capitalism in Indonesia from 1870 to 1914, as with those of the Culture System at an earlier date, appear, on superficial inspection, unambiguous. Production and export of a whole range of commodities, including some new to Indonesia's trade, rose dramatically. The area planted with sugar increased fourfold, while output rose ninefold. Tobacco production, which had averaged $8\frac{1}{2}$ million kilogrammes per annum in the period 1865 to 1869, reached 65 million kgs. annually in the years just before the First World War. Over the same period, tea production jumped from $1\frac{1}{2}$ m. kgs. to 25 m. per annum. Important new products made their appearance—including rubber, oil and its by-products, cinchona (the bark from which quinine—once so important in the treatment of malaria—is extracted), cassava (a root crop—widely used in the diet locally—from which tapioca is obtained, and which is used in the manufacture of cattle food, cheap brandy, adhesives, sizes, and paper), and copra (the dried 'meat' of the coconut, from which vegetable oil is extracted for a wide variety of uses).

Moreover, with certain products the Netherlands East Indies succeeded in virtually cornering the market, supplying, for example, over 90 per cent of the world's cinchona, and 70-80 per cent of its cassava and kapok (a fibre used for stuffing cushions, pillows, etc., and in the manufacture of equipment—such as life-jackets—in which lightness and buoyancy are important). This success was the outcome of close co-operation between government, agricultural research institutes, planters, and marketing organizations.

The capital and, to some extent, the estate management which contributed to this economic 'miracle' were international. Nearly half the capital invested in the Indonesian rubber industry in 1912 was British, and the tea industry, too, owed much to British capital and experience (and consumption). German, French, Belgian, Swedish, American, and other countries' investors and adventurers all played their part. Dutch capital retained its historical hold in Java, but in the scramble for the wealth of the Outer Islands free trade and economic liberalism meant that it was only one contender among many.

The developments of this period, while in a sense assimilating the Outer Islands administratively to the condition of Java, at the same time accentuated the differences between them in other respects.

In the first place, it was clearly necessary to establish *Rust en Orde* (peace and quiet) in the Outer Islands, just as it had been established in Java, before an appropriate climate for investment could be secured. The decades before 1870 had already witnessed purposeful Dutch attempts to establish firmer administrative control outside Java, and this process was now accelerated. The major obstacle to the extension of Dutch authority was the Sumatran state of Atjeh, against which operations were first launched in 1873. It took over thirty years, an expenditure of 400 million guilders, and the loss of countless lives, before it could be claimed that it had been pacified. Dutch writ now ran over virtually the whole area known today as Indonesia.

But the history and contemporary circumstances of the Outer Islands ensured divergence from the experience of Java, not least in the economic sphere. Dutch measures reducing mortality (road and railway construction lessening the risk of famine, vaccination against smallpox, other public health measures, imposition of internal security) had swollen population in Java, forcing concentration upon subsistence food production on the available land not already taken by the big Dutch plantations. Moreover, Javanese economic initiative had been stultified by compulsory cultivation and forced labour, and by the entrenched economic power of the Chinese and other alien groups.

Things were different elsewhere and allowed some Indonesians to take advantage of the burgeoning economic opportunities. Land was in general more plentiful, and it was easier to integrate cultivation of commercial crops with the *ladang* (extensive) system of food production than with *sawah* production of wet rice (the obvious commercial crop in the latter case was sugar, but government regulations forbade the sugar factories to process 'native' cane, which was thus relegated to the production of poor-quality brown sugar for the local market). Furthermore, some of the Outer Islands, particularly Sumatra, had retained direct outside trading links with the world, and had not suffered the withering of economic initiative characteristic of Java.

Statistics measure the consequences of the opening up of the Outer Islands. Their share of total Indonesian exports rose from about 22 per cent in the eighteen-seventies to 44 per cent in the years immediately preceding the First World War. The old consumption crops—such as coffee, sugar, and tea—in which Western, and especially Dutch, capital had a stranglehold, were predominantly Java-grown. The new raw material crops and products, such as tin, petroleum, rubber, and copra were, in contrast, predominantly based on the Outer Islands. Where large capital sums and sophisticated technologies were required, as in the case of petroleum, Western enterprise naturally monopolized development. But where it was possible for the smallholder to enter the field, he seized the opportunity with alacrity. In 1910 Indonesian smallholders were credited with 70 per cent of the export value of agricultural products shipped from the Outer Islands. In the face of the Western investment boom this share later fell—to around the 40 per cent mark—but it was nevertheless a considerable achievement.

Finally, in assessing the credit record of the 1870-1914 period, we should note the changes in Dutch policy towards welfare and social capital provision during these years. In 1878 the *Batig Slot* (Indies contribution to the Dutch Treasury), which Van den Bosch had inaugurated in 1831, came to an end. In forty-eight years it had contributed a total of some 832.4 million guilders to Holland's exchequer. Instead, expenditures in Indonesia itself began to exceed revenues raised there. Up to 1900 250 million guilders were spent on building railways, extending the irrigation system, constructing harbours, and on other such purposes. This represented the essential social capital counterpart and supplement to the huge influx of private capital (into plantations, mines, banks, insurance companies, and other appurtenances of economic development) which characterized the pre-First World War decades.

In the field of welfare, a beginning was made, albeit modest, in the provision of educational and health facilities for the Indonesian people. It has been said that, in proposing a policy of expenditure for these purposes from the home treasury, the Netherlands was many years ahead of other colonial powers. This is true. Britain made a start in 1929 with the Colonial Development Act (which provided up to £1 million a year). Holland bettered this by twenty-five years (and the initial grant made in 1904 was worth over £3 million). The new attitude of the Dutch towards their colony has been called the 'Ethical Policy'.

But Dutch motives were mixed. There *were* humanitarians in Holland, and their influence was important. But what they urged would not have gained more general acceptance had it not corresponded with needs felt by those possessed of altogether less praiseworthy motives.

At first, every circumstance had favoured private enterprise. Prices of primary products continued to rise in the early eighteen-seventies. But then they began generally to fall, and in the mid-eighteen-eighties the terms of trade also turned against primary producers— that is to say that food and raw material prices began to fall faster than the prices of manufactured goods, so that producers of the former had to export more in order to be able to import an unchanged quantity of the latter. To complicate matters for the planter, coffee disease first made its appearance on the estates of Java in 1878, and sugar-cane was attacked by disease in 1882. Finally, at the moment of crisis in the mid-eighteen-eighties, many of the recently—and hastily—opened agricultural banks failed.

One of the most important consequences of this crisis was the replacement of most private planters by big corporations. These had head-offices in Holland, ran their huge estates in Indonesia through appointed managers, and enjoyed far greater financial security. The corporations in turn naturally exerted a correspondingly greater pressure and influence on government, and their sheer size and power themselves contributed to the intensification of colonial exploitation.

The corporations were not prepared to provide from their own resources the roads, railways, harbours, and irrigation systems they increasingly needed. Nor did they wish to pay taxes which would significantly contribute to the cost. It was for this reason that the Indies contribution to the Dutch exchequer ceased, as the cost of capital construction of that kind had to be met by borrowing and by running deficits on the colonial budget. Later, when politicians and public in Holland came to realize that as a result of three decades of capitalism in Indonesia the living standards of the people of the archipelago were actually declining, it was felt that a positive contribution to their welfare had to be made.

But even the social services—educational and health primarily—resulting from the Ethical Policy were, in the words of a Dutch scholar '. . . strongly subject to the influence of the powerful estate companies and other large-scale enterprises. Irrigation measures benefited the sugar concerns as much as the agricultural population. The health service was, in part, closely related to the need of the various enterprises for physically fit labour. The fight against contagious diseases, such as plague and cholera, was a direct gain for Western business. In so far as it exceeded the elementary instruction of the *desa* schools [village, vernacular] education mainly provided training for administrative personnel in the service of government and business. The road system and the experimental stations existed chiefly for the benefit of the plantations.'

And, in any case, we must ask whose was the

responsibility for 'diminishing welfare' in the first place? That the welfare of the Javanese at least was declining at this time is not in dispute, since it was the Dutch Queen herself who announced in 1901 her government's intention to 'enquire into the diminishing welfare of the people of Java'.

The factors involved in this deplorable outcome of a century of Dutch economic activity were many. The population of Indonesia increased dramatically—from 6 million people in 1800 to 38 million in 1900—as a result of Dutch *Rust en Orde*. But little—if anything at all, deliberately and directly that is—was done to create job opportunities commensurate with the numbers involved and appropriate to the need. Manufacturing industry in Holland would like to have seen Indonesian incomes raised—every grocer knows that rich customers are preferable to poor ones—but on the other hand had no desire to see competitive industries arising in Indonesia, industries which would have afforded local employment of a kind contributing to the right climate and circumstances for general economic development. The big Dutch estate and mining concerns with interests in Indonesia, on the other hand, had no objection to certain kinds of 'service' industries (machinery repairs, breweries, soft drink manufactories, etc.) arising on the spot, but had a clear interest in depressing the wages paid to Indonesians to the lowest possible level—to bare subsistence or even below. In the Jogjakarta region before the agricultural reform of 1918 the minimum wage was virtually zero, since labour was recruited compulsorily by the Dutch sugar companies, stepping into the shoes of the traditional rulers, and not paid.

On overcrowded Java, the great sugar concerns competed with the peasants for the best land, regulated the irrigation systems in their own favour, kept the *sawah* under sugar for longer than they were entitled to and thereby forced the peasants to grow faster-ripening crops with lower nutritional value than rice, and in a host of other ways disrupted and damaged the life of the Javanese villagers. And behind the sugar companies, ultimately, lay the power of the government.

But even on the other islands, the economic opportunities we have referred to—the chance for Indonesian smallholders to turn to commercial crops—were not a simple net benefit, for marketing was frequently controlled by the Chinese and other middleman groups, while Dutch shippers often penalized the smallholder with discriminatory freight rates—that is, in effect, pocketed part of the profits of the smallholders' efforts. Where others—the Western companies and the Chinese —already had economic power and influence, it was extremely difficult for the local peoples to break in and establish themselves on an equal or competitive footing.

Moreover, for many Indonesians the opening up of big new enterprises in the Outer Islands by Western capital meant only a chance to toil in them as coolie labour. Since people were over-plentiful on Java and in short supply on islands such as Sumatra, Coolie Ordinances were passed enabling agents to recruit on the one to ship to the other. The most notorious provision of these Ordinances was that known as the Penal Sanction. Coolies guilty of (or deemed by the employer or his agents guilty of) breach of contract or laziness were liable to punishment. A writer who had himself been a planter notes of these contract workers that: 'They may not run away from their work for that is forbidden by their contract which the ignorant, misled coolie signed somewhere in Java. . . . They are doing forced labour, or, if you like, they are slaves. The coolie slogs from morning till night, toiling and stooping; he has to stand up to the neck in stinking marshland, while

greedy leeches suck his thin blood and malaria mos-
quitoes poison his sickly body. But he cannot run away;
for the contract binds him. The *tjentengs*, the watch-
men and constables of the firm, who have the strength
of giants and are bestially cruel, track down the fugitive.
When they catch him, they give him a terrible hiding
and lock him up, for the contract binds him.' The coolie
rarely worked off his debts—the employer and his shops
and his credit saw to that. To raise a little ready cash,
the coolie could, of course, sell his wife to a white man
to be his *nyay* (woman) for ten guilders or so.

Finally, as far as the imposition of *Rust en Orde* was
concerned, time showed that this was not simply for the
purpose of facilitating Western investment, but also to
protect it once established from the rising forces of
nationalism, socialism, and communism. For this purpose, the integration of the traditional rulers and hereditary chiefs and leaders into the administration, so that
they were cut off from the people in terms of interests
and position, was an obvious move, depriving indigenous society as it did of its natural élite.

It might be thought that in the foregoing the
emphasis has been too exclusively economic. In a sense
this is true, but nevertheless it accurately reflects the
predominant and overriding Dutch interest in their
colony—profit. Such a narrowly commercial concern
naturally provoked a hostile and increasingly violent
response among the Indonesian victims. Many of the
grievances were economic in origin. Others arose from
the daily humiliations of life as second or third class
citizens in their own country. From the growing aware-
ness and articulation of these grievances arose the
modern Indonesian nationalist movement which gath-
ered momentum through the course of the first five
decades of the 20th century.

Resistance to the Dutch 'forward movement' by

which the outer islands were effectively incorporated into the Indies administration flared fitfully in the late 19th and early 20th centuries. Between 1903 and 1908, for example, wars against Dutch domination were fought in South and North Sumatra, South and Central Celebes, Borneo, and Bali. Twice in Bali Dutch troops 'were confronted by rulers, who, facing defeat and deserted by the mass of their people, preferred to die fighting rather than to submit. Surrounded by their families and followers, all armed with spear and *kris*, the rulers flung themselves on the Dutch guns until all—men, women and children—were wiped out.' The equation between colonization and violence drawn by African writer Frantz Fanon can be tragically illustrated from the history of Dutch power in Indonesia.

But a successful *national* movement for independence had to have roots different from those spasmodic local risings. It is true that rural discontent was widespread. Everything conspired to increase the peasant's need for cash: to meet tax demands (three-quarters of taxation was collected from Indonesians—the poorest section of the community); to light the house with a kerosene lamp; to buy salt from the government monopoly; to buy cigarettes and fish; and to buy some of the coveted manufactured goods imported from the West and Japan. To raise cash, more and more of the peasants leased their land to rice merchants or moneylenders, continuing to work the land themselves as sharecroppers or sub-tenants and handing over from one half to five-sevenths of the crop to the absentee lessee. But the resulting rural distress and unrest was in large measure inarticulate and fragmentary. These people were mostly illiterate, and frequently deprived too of their own natural local spokesmen by the bribery of the plantations or the needs of the administration.

However, a new class was arising that *was* articulate

and national—the Western-educated, white-collar, in-digenous bourgeoisie. Western businesses and the Indies administration required some trained Indonesians, and small numbers succeeded in attaining university and professional qualifications in Indonesia or abroad. In the process, they could not but come into contact with dis-turbing and suggestive ideas—ideas, for example, such as national self-determination, democracy, and social-ism. Nor could they help but observe the progress of nationalism in other Asian countries such as India, Japan, and China. Japan was particularly exciting, since it had avoided colonialism and succeeded in becoming a modern industrial power—and one strong enough to beat white Russia on land and at sea in the war of 1904-1905. It would be hard to exaggerate the importance of these Japanese victories for the development of nation-alism throughout colonial Asia.

These indigenous élites were privileged as compared with the rural peasantry. Nonetheless, they too were dissatisfied with their lot under colonialism. Even where they had equal or better qualifications, they were paid less than Dutchmen doing the same job. They were discriminated against in a dozen ways. And they had no say in their own government.

A third element in the Indonesian nationalist move-ment consisted of Indonesian small businessmen or would-be businessmen. In this case there tended to be a strong connection with Islam and the *santri* tradition. This arose in part from the mode of Islam's transmis-sion to and through the archipelago. But it was also a function of the opportunities and circumstances of some of the outer islands, notably Sumatra. Here Islam had its strongest foothold, and here too were the economic opportunities for smallholder enterprise in a host of commercial crops. Moreover, Dutch policy, by favour-ing the traditional secular leaders as against the religious dignitaries, made the latter the obvious rallying points for nationalist aspirations.

The grievances of the indigenous business community were real. Where production was in their own hands, marketing was frequently in the control of Chinese or other alien middlemen, with final shipping controlled by Europeans. In this way, as much as half of the market price might be lost to the Indonesian producer. Other economic opportunities were denied to the indigenous peoples by the stranglehold already procured by those with more capital and greater economic experience behind them. In the *batik* industry, as the market extended from the immediate locality to the archipelago as a whole, it was the Chinese who stepped in and increased the scale of operations. They established workshops, supplied the raw materials to local workers, and finally purchased and distributed the finished product. In this larger-scale operation, the Chinese replaced locally-made cloth by cheaper mass-produced imported cloth, thus destroying a local subsidiary industry in the process. An official inquiry carried out as early as 1892 showed that the whole *batik* industry had thus passed into Chinese hands 'with the native workmen reduced to a position of dependence often approaching slavery'.

Similarly, although cassava was grown by Indonesians, most of the tapioca mills were Chinese; the cleaning and pressing of kapok developed as an Indonesian industry, but soon passed into Chinese hands; and the

---

3. Terraced rice fields in the Priangan mountains, West Java. Note how the low dykes restraining the irrigation water follow the hill contours.
4. *Architecture old and new*
   (a) Batak house for sixteen families, Sumatra.
   (b) The Ministry of Trade building in Djkarta. Note how the architectural treatment makes for coolness and shade in the interior of the building.

4a

4b

rice mills and plant for the preparation of copra and coconut oil were also predominantly Chinese. The European shipping companies obtained their share of the profits of indigenous enterprises by manipulating freight rates. For example, freight rates were raised on tapioca, cultivation of which was almost entirely in Indonesian hands; this, commented the Annual Report of the Java Bank, 1913-14, '. . . works as an indirect tax on the native, a tax however by which not the community at large but only a few privileged ones will benefit'.

In these circumstances, it was hardly surprising that one of the earliest nationalist movements was in fact a Society of Muslim Traders—*Sarekat Dagang Islam*—founded in 1911, to sponsor national trade interests. Earlier, in 1908, a cultural association—*Budi Utomo* ('Noble Endeavour')—had been set up by Indonesian intellectuals (mostly Javanese *prijaji*) opposed to colonial oppression. From these beginnings, the nationalist movement made rapid progress. In 1912 *Sarekat Dagang Islam* became simply *Sarekat Islam*, an avowedly political movement, and by 1919 it had enrolled the support of over two million members, including of course large numbers of peasants as well as the indigenous nationalist élites.

Such a rapid development thoroughly alarmed the Dutch, especially in view of their own position—

5. *Activities traditional and modern*
    (a) Wood-carving on the island of Bali. Note the head-dresses.
    (b) Young research students learning how to control malaria.
6. *Staples of the Indonesian economy*
    (a) A young woman *batik* worker applies wax to outline the design on a *sarong*. *Batik*, apart from its universal use in Indonesia, is world famous and much sought after.
    (b) A typical coastal scene. With over 28,000 miles of coast, Indonesia's fishing industry is an important sector of the economy.

rendered precarious by the circumstances of the First World War. Their response was twofold—token concessions to moderate opinion, and ruthless repression of effective leaders and 'extremist elements'. In the first category was the inception of a *Volksraad* (People's Council) in 1918. This was basically an advisory body. The existence of appointed as well as elected members, the extremely limited franchise upon which its membership was based, and the indirect form of the elections to it guaranteed that Europeans formed a majority. Subsequent reforms did little to change its status, and it remained an inadequate vehicle for nationalist aspirations. Action in the second category included imprisonment and exile of suspects: as early as 1913 the three leaders of the 'Indian Party', founded in 1912 with the stated objective of complete national independence for Indonesia, were exiled.

Whatever the Dutch view at the time, the appearance of irresistible progress of the nationalist movement during *Sarekat Islam*'s heyday was something of an illusion. 'The nationalist movement' consisted essentially of a coalition of indigenous social classes, and their divergent interests and values soon led to fragmentation and controversy. We will see later how Japanese occupation followed by war against the Dutch forged Indonesian national unity—for a time (though in independent Indonesia the divergent interests of the different social strata again led to the breakdown of consensus). The inter-war period, however, was to prove one in which political organizations proliferated in Indonesia, and in which the casualty rate among such organizations was extremely high.

A major and obvious impediment to united action was that the most articulate leadership available to the nationalist movement was largely Western-oriented and urban, while the vast mass of the people were rural and those prominent among them—the richer peasants, the religious functionaries—were inclined to be tradition-orientated (poor peasants must always have at least a revolutionary *potential*, such is the oppression they suffer). In the early years of *Sarekat Islam* enthusiasm concealed the heterogeneity of the elements drawn from all indigenous social classes by the rallying symbol of Islam, and for a short time the nationalist élite were able to make contact with the rural people. Thereafter, Dutch policy and disagreements inside the élite itself combined to disrupt this co-operation. The Indies government deliberately sought by restrictions and repression to prevent the urban leaders from proselytizing in the rural areas. At the same time, an important section of the nationalist leadership was embracing radical political ideas suspect to the more conservative and religiously-minded rural leaders.

Actually, in the broadest sense there was fairly general agreement in all sections of the Indonesian nationalist movement on the need for 'socialism': controversy concerned the kind of socialism and the means by which it could or should be brought about. The reasons for such agreement were complex. In the first place, colonialism, seen as the basic cause of all the contemporary misfortunes of Indonesia, was identified with capitalism. For the literate, there was justification for accepting this identification in the writings of European socialists, especially those influenced by Marxism-Leninism. Even small Indonesian businessmen could be against big or 'sinful' capitalism, since it was big 'sinful' capitalism in the hands of Chinese and Europeans which blocked economic opportunities for the indigenous people. In the second place, modernist Islamic ideas as adapted in Indonesia gave rise to a kind of religious socialism somewhat akin to Christian socialism in Britain. Finally, it was widely felt that capitalism, with its accent on individualism and competition, was incompatible with the traditional values of Indonesian life such as *gotong rojong*.

However, the differences in accent and emphasis of the various groups was enough to cause discord. The left-wing groups formed the Communist Party of the Indies (*Perserikaten Kommunis di India* or P.K.I.; later *Partai Komunis Indonesia*) in 1920, and *Sarekat Islam* split soon afterwards, very much along *santri-prijaji-abangan* lines—corresponding to right/left alignment. The communists increasingly concentrated on the urban workers and other wage-earners, but serious unrest continued in the rural areas, from time to time erupting in physical violence, as it had in Celebes and West Java in 1919.

The reasons were not hard to seek. Indonesian real incomes started to decline in 1914, and continued to fall until 1924. The war brought difficulties. Shipping was in short supply, and rice imports difficult. This situation happened to coincide with a series of bad harvests, and the government instituted highly unpopular compulsory grain collections at fixed prices. Despite the critical food situation—the region of Kediri in Java suffered famine and troops had to be sent in to crush protest—the sugar companies, anticipating high prices, refused to release land for rice. As a result, peasants in the sugar districts resorted to violence, setting fire to cane fields. Things were no better for wage-earners at the time. A government report concluded that their incomes were too low to provide a 'hygienically sufficient means of existence' (i.e. they were starving).

The inter-war years were in general economically disturbed and detrimental to the interests of the colonial peoples. First warning of underlying problems of a serious nature came with the brief but sharp slump of the years 1920 and 1921. Thereafter it seemed as if the pre-war expansion and development of primary production was to continue 'normally' in the post-war world, having worked the war and its aftermath out of the system. True, primary product prices began to decline after 1925, but continuing growth in the volume of exports tended to mask this. Then came the 1929 economic 'crash', which precipitated a disastrous collapse in prices. Recovery began from the mid-thirties, but was incomplete until the coming war threw its shadow ahead in the form of a sharp rise in demand for strategic raw materials for stock-piling.

In attempting to assess the impact of these fluctuations on Indonesia, it is again necessary to resort to credit and debit entries, although for a time at the depth of the Depression almost all was debit. However, not all was net loss. There *was* some growth of manufacturing industry during this period, for example. There had been a modest, and temporary, burst of activity in this direction during the First World War, in order to make good some of the deficiencies caused by partial severance from Europe. But afterwards much of the mushroom development was allowed to relapse. Attempts to encourage industry in the thirties sprang from two factors: one, the failure of Indonesia's exports to earn sufficient to buy what had come to be the desired level of manufactured imports; and, two, the fear that cheap Japanese manufactured imports would corner the Indies economy. Behind a barrier of tariffs, quotas, and other restrictions, the Indies government extended cautious support to a handful of what we would now call 'import-substitution' industries, while local enterprise also took advantage of this protection to extend its activities. For example, the manufacture of locally-produced cigarettes increased rapidly between 1933 and 1937, the value of output rising from about 1 million guilders to about 9 million—some of it taking place in small factories.

Another industry was the manufacture of plaited hats, both for local sale and for export.

Indonesian smallholders at first profited greatly from circumstances. Britain's decision to restrict rubber production unilaterally in her colonies after 1922, in order to raise prices, in fact afforded producers in the Indies a golden opportunity for expansion, and it was accepted. Production of rubber in the archipelago almost trebled between 1920 and 1930, and more than half was in smallholder (i.e. local) hands. Even when the Depression struck rubber prices—they had reached 4/8 per lb. in 1925, and touched $3\frac{1}{2}$d. per lb. in 1930—the smallholders proved that they had much greater powers of flexibility and adaptability than the big European plantations. However, deliberate steps were taken officially to favour the latter.

The increased money incomes in the hands of those Indonesians profiting from commercial crop production, together with the appearance of an embryo indigenous manufacturing sector, also encouraged the development of an indigenous trading sector. The most important group involved in this trade in Java were devout Muslims drawn from the north coast regions and Madura, and handling dried fish, local cigarettes, leather goods, cheap textiles, soap, and the like.

Until the collapse of the sugar boom, too, a certain amount of benefit seeped out from the giant European enterprises to the local people. This took the form of land rent paid for the areas under sugar, and the wages paid to local employees. Of the estimated value of the 1927-28 sugar harvest, for example—400 million guilders —about 134 million guilders went in rents and wages. In these circumstances, it might have been anticipated that something like an enterprising rural 'gentry' might have arisen.

What did in practice happen leads us naturally into

the debits. First, when the crash came—the price of sugar fell from 25/- a cwt in the early nineteen-twenties to 5/- a cwt in the mid-thirties, and the area under sugar from almost 700,000 acres in 1931 to 67,000 in 1935—rents and wages fell away almost to nothing, and the minute compensation paid by the sugar enterprises for cancellation of contracts went into the hands only of the richer and more powerful peasants and landlords. Second, even during the boom years, Dutch policy, influenced by the European producers, discouraged cane-growing among the Indonesian landowners, and this, in effect, favoured the growth of a 'rentier' class—relying upon the rents paid for their land from the foreign companies—rather than an enterprising 'gentry' class, who might have laid foundations for autonomous economic growth. Overall, the inter-war years saw a continued polarization of Indonesian rural society, especially on Java, where about two-thirds of the population came to be landless peasants, coolies or poor peasants. Those who succeeded in raising themselves to middle- or rich-peasant status were frequently *santri*.

As far as smallholders were concerned, government measures taken to counteract the effects of falling prices were unsatisfactory. This was especially marked under the 1934 International Rubber Restriction Agreement, which imposed penal export taxes on smallholder rubber and, in effect, prevented the small indigenous grower from re-planting or increasing his acreage. Indonesian nationalists saw the Restriction scheme as a means whereby smallholders were punished for growing rubber efficiently, while high-cost white estates were protected.

The violent fluctuations of the inter-war years exacerbated the problems faced by the embryo indigenous 'capitalists', whether smallholders or traders, in establishing themselves against the entrenched Chinese and

Europeans. But for the mass of the people conditions were, with brief respite perhaps in the boom years of 1925-28, truly deplorable. The average diet was poorer at the end of the nineteen-thirties than it had been at the start of the century. Population continued to increase rapidly, and for the greater part had to be absorbed in an already congested subsistence sector. For those who had found wage employment in the mine and plantation sector during the boom years, the Depression meant returning to their villages or swelling the ranks of unemployed poor in the towns and cities.

It emerges very clearly from League of Nations and other statistics that few countries in the world suffered so severely from the inter-war economic breakdown of capitalism as Indonesia, because of the extraordinary degree of specialization on the production of a handful of vulnerable export crops. Moreover, whereas the working classes of the industrial Western countries had some protection against the economic blizzard, in the form of strong trade unions and some welfare services such as unemployment and health insurance, the working classes of colonial countries like Indonesia had nothing. (Average real incomes in Britain were actually higher in 1939 than they had been in 1919; the same could certainly not be said of Indonesia.) Unions were weak and fragmented along political lines, and in view of the massive unemployment and underemployment powerless to afford their members any kind of protection. And far from the Indies government creating a welfare 'umbrella' to protect the people of the archipelago, expenditures were drastically reduced in step with the fall of prices and resulting fall in revenue.

As one would expect in view of the economic turmoil, the inter-war years witnessed an intensification of nationalist struggle. This was reflected at a number of levels. In the early nineteen-twenties there were several waves of strikes, some of them violent. These culminated in the PKI instigated revolts of 1926 (West Java) and 1927 (West Sumatra). All these manifestations of revolutionary despair were easily crushed by the Dutch, who in response severely tightened up their regulations governing such rights as those of assembly, freedom of speech, and a free press. One result was that, convinced that nothing was to be achieved by political action, '. . . the Indonesian masses retired from the stage, not to return until Japan's victory over the Dutch proved once and for all that the white ruler was not invincible'.

But at another level, preparation for eventual independence went on. A group of younger nationalist leaders arose who in time became responsible for the new state after the Second World War, among them the future President—Sukarno. These tended to be generally secular in outlook—less influenced by Islam than their predecessors. They also described themselves generally as socialists, if not Marxists, but were far more closely nationalist in orientation and interests than the leaders of the PKI (which had virtually disappeared as an organized force after the 1926-27 débâcle). Unfortunately, intense Dutch repression, involving all the prominent leaders in long spells of exile and imprisonment, prevented the formation of any single strong unifying party such as the National Congress of British India. Moreover, Dutch security vigilance, combined with the post-1926-27 apathy of the people, prevented these leaders from forging strong links with the country's peasantry. The new leaders did however study and articulate many of the economic injustices and hardships which afflicted their country.

It was from groups of Indonesian students and recent graduates, some from the Netherlands, that the new leaders emerged. The *Perhimpunan Indonesia*, or Indonesian Union (of Indonesian students in Holland), had been highly influential for some years when, in 1927, a group of them having returned to Indonesia, they joined with a Bandung student and graduate group led by a young engineer called Sukarno to form the Indonesian Nationalist Party (PNI). The success of this party, which demanded complete independence (and in the meantime non-cooperation with the Dutch), led in a couple of years to the arrest of most of its leaders and its suppression. Sukarno was imprisoned from 1929 to 1932. On his release, he found the Indonesian nationalist movement plagued by its usual weakness—fragmentation. No single party could establish itself as the true successor of the PNI. Then in 1933 Sukarno was arrested again and exiled. Next year two of his most prominent colleagues followed him into exile—Hatta and Sjahrir. All three, and many more, were to spend the best part of the next ten years festering in remote parts of the archipelago until released by the Japanese invaders.

Frustrated in its directly political expression, the nationalist aspiration manifested itself now in a variety of 'self-help' activities. The Islamic reform organization Muhammadijah set up its own schools, cooperatives and clinics. So did its more traditionalist and rural-based Islamic rival Nahdatul Ulama. Other nationalists concentrated on journalism and cultural activities. Their work was rewarded in the artistic flowering of the revolutionary period in the nineteen-forties, with the appearance of major Indonesian writers such as the poet Chairil Anwar. It was also necessary to win general acceptance of *Bahasa* among the people—a people so divided by tongues. It is to Sukarno's credit that he was one of the first to realize the national potential of *Bahasa*; he thus helped to spare independent Indonesia the language troubles of Ceylon, India, Malaysia and other new nations.

Developments in Indonesia from 1900 onwards con-

spired in the end to harden reaction among the Dutch
community in the Indies. Those who had genuinely
approached the Ethical Policy with altruistic, albeit
paternalistic, intentions had had to face the scepticism
of the more 'realistic'. The latter were, not unnaturally,
only too ready to see the violent upheavals of the nineteen-twenties as evidence of the 'ungratefulness' of the
'native', and as proof that only repressive policies could
work. Mass arrests and banishments, executions, and
all the apparatus of a police state became the order of
the day. More or less liberal Governors-General were
replaced by one who said, in 1936, 'we have ruled here
for 300 years with the whip and the club and we shall
still be doing it in another 300 years'. A number of
overtly and explicitly fascist clubs arose among the
Dutch settlers in the Indies. It was over a tense uneasy
truce that the Pacific War loomed.

The approaching struggle found the nationalists, as
usual, divided. Some were frankly admirers of the
Japanese achievement, and had studied in Japan. Others
saw the struggle through the filter of Marxism and pro-
moted the defeat of fascism above the attainment of
national independence in the list of priorities. From
those, and from others of moderate political ambitions,
came demands that the Dutch should arm the Indonesian people in defence of their country. This the
Dutch would not do. They had traditionally drawn
their local troops from Christianized minority groups,
such as the Ambonese and Minahasans, and had
extended the privilege of service with their army to only
a handful of others; very few Indonesians had risen
from the ranks.

Even the German invasion of Holland failed to rouse
the Indies Dutch from their traditional attitudes. When
the Japanese reached the archipelago early in 1942,
their victory was sensationally swift and complete.

Those Europeans who failed to escape were rounded up, publicly humiliated, and interned for the duration of the war. Many who did succeed in escaping did so by abandoning all the standards that had governed their lives as colonialists: 'I watched them,' subsequently wrote a (Western) eye-witness, 'running for their lives as the news spread that the Japanese had landed . . . I watched them as they threw away their uniforms or whatever else they wore, and donned native clothing and stained their faces brown.' The Dutch master race could never—nor ever did—recover from its disgrace and dishonour. This in itself was one of the most important consequences of the Japanese invasion for the Indonesian nationalists. The mass of the people had seen at last that the Emperor had no clothes.

But there were many other consequences, so many and of such magnitude that they completely transformed the situation, and with it the prospects for Indonesian independence. The nationalist leaders, released from banishment, agreed to split forces. Sukarno and Hatta were to work with the Japanese, with a view to extracting whatever concessions could be obtained from them. Others, including Sjahrir, went underground to organize and prepare for the envisaged independence.

The advantages of this arrangement were many. It is true that Sukarno and Hatta had to play the anti-imperialist, anti-white, anti-Western tune dictated by the Japanese. On the other hand, the tune could very readily be adapted to Indonesian nationalist purposes by a speaker as skilful and polyglot as Sukarno, and as the war advanced he left less and less doubt in the minds of his listeners that his anti-imperialism extended to the Japanese imperialists too. Further, the Japanese eventually permitted propagation of the national language, use of the Indonesian flag, and singing of the Indonesian national anthem. These important symbols of nationhood were familiarized from one end of the archipelago to the other by Sukarno and Hatta.

Sjahrir and the others in the underground were meanwhile laying the framework for an organization that would be capable of resisting the return of the Dutch. In other ways, too, the Indonesian people were undergoing a crash course in readiness for their coming struggle for freedom. The Japanese created a large number of quasi-military organizations, especially among youth. They also latterly established Indonesian-officered armies. In this way large numbers of people learned to shoot straight—an important, if not vital, accomplishment for those seeking national liberation. Again, as the unpopularity of Japanese rule alienated more and more of the people—hundreds of thousands of Indonesians were sent abroad for slave labour, while those who escaped this impressment faced inflation, famine, and the depredations of an inhuman secret police—armed clashes grew increasingly frequent, especially in the last year of the occupation, when the eye-witness cited above claims that Indonesians, fiercely bent on revenge, killed the Japanese by the hundreds.

Another important outcome of the Japanese occupation was that it enabled large numbers of Indonesians to acquire administrative experience which they would never otherwise have obtained. The Dutch had jealously preserved the highest, decision-making, posts for their own nationals, and their failure to train a body of Indonesians for ultimate national responsibility, besides being one of the major blemishes in their colonial record, accurately mirrored their determination to stay on in Indonesia as the masters. The Japanese, on the other hand, required the services of hundreds of Indonesians, who suddenly found themselves thrust into positions of authority.

Although the Japanese from the start talked about

granting independence to Indonesia, as to other South-East Asian countries, this 'independence' was originally envisaged in the context of the 'Greater East Asia Co-Prosperity Sphere', by which Japan planned to secure East, South, and South-East Asia as a closed market for her manufactured goods and as a hinterland to supply her with food and raw materials. (Japan's imperial adventure was to some extent forced upon her by the actions of the Western colonial powers—such as Holland —in trying to exclude her economically from this area.) As the war wore on, however, and defeat became inevitable and imminent, a number of concrete steps were taken to advance Indonesian independence.

In March 1945 the Japanese appointed a joint committee, the majority of which was Indonesian, to discuss plans for independence. Although general agreement was reached on the basic political principles which should guide the future Indonesian nation, there were not wanting signs of deep-rooted differences of opinion. The Japanese, by welding Muhammadijah and Nahdatul Ulama into a single body, Masjumi, and by encouraging competition between it and the more secular leadership, such as Sukarno's, had sharpened pre-existing stresses. It was Sukarno's famous speech expounding his *Pantja Sila* ('five foundations'; five basic principles) which enabled an uneasy compromise to be made between those who advocated a straightforward Muslim theocratic state and the others who favoured secularism. The *Pantja Sila* were: nationalism (*kebangsaan*); internationalism, or humanitarianism (*perikemanusiaan*); democracy, or representation (*kerakjatan*); social justice (*keadilan sosial*); and faith in one God (*ke-Tuhanan*, or *pengakuan ke-Tuhanan Jang Maha-Esa*).

On 7 August 1945 the Japanese authorized the establishment of an all-Indonesian Independence Preparatory Committee with Sukarno as Chairman and Hatta as

Vice-Chairman, and entrusted it with the task of arranging to take over government. When the Japanese surrendered a week later, Sukarno and Hatta proclaimed independence within three days, on 17 August 1945. Next day Sukarno became President of the Republic of Indonesia, and Hatta Vice-President.

Before describing the ensuing struggle against the returning Dutch, a word or two should be added about the Japanese period. Repressive and tyrannical though their rule was, the Japanese rulers were not all tyrants. A number genuinely were in favour of, and worked for, Indonesian independence; some stayed on after the war to fight on the side of the nationalists against the Dutch. Others, in pursuit of the Imperial policy of local self-sufficiency, fostered a certain amount of light industry, including textiles (with the concomitant cotton cultivation), and some effort was made to advise villagers in Japanese rice-growing methods, which, had they been universally adopted, would have very greatly raised Javanese yields. These things were however over-shadowed by the violence and insolence that character-ized Japanese rule.

The Dutch were not prepared to accept the new Republic, which they regarded as a Japanese puppet régime. In this they were mistaken, since all elements in Indonesian life, including the former underground units, rallied to its cause. Only a handful of aristocrats and other hereditary leaders who had become too closely associated with the Dutch in the pre-war period held off, and in Sumatra and elsewhere popular upris-ings, often led by religious leaders, killed or expelled large numbers of these. Arms came chiefly from Japan-ese sources, either willingly supplied or forcibly seized.

The British, to whom had been entrusted the task of taking the Japanese surrender and restoring law and order, arrived in Java in late September. The Dutch quickly followed, and fighting spluttered throughout the archipelago. The military struggle followed a pattern which was to become all too familiar in the postwar world. The colonial power succeeded in seizing and holding the major urban areas, but failed to control or hold the countryside and communications systems. Nevertheless, the Dutch were by no means militarily defeated when, eventually, they gave in and recognized Indonesian independence. It was the interaction of other factors which in the end proved decisive.

First, internal developments helped to recommend the Republic to Western opinion. Late in 1945 government changes increased the influence of the former underground leaders, such as Sjahrir, at the expense of those who had 'collaborated' with the Japanese (though it should be noted that it was precisely the collaborators whom the Americans had restored to power in the neighbouring Philippines). At the same time decision-making processes became more democratic. Then in 1948 an abortive communist-led coup was suppressed by the Republican forces, and many communist leaders were killed in battle or subsequently executed. Western governments, especially the United States, had expressed growing concern at the extension of communist influence in the Republican-held areas; this evidence of anti-communism was especially welcome in view of the contemporary victories being registered by the communists in China. In general, those Republicans who favoured compromise and negotiation with the Dutch retained the upper hand against the more intransigent left.

Second, Dutch actions were simultaneously alienating world opinion and isolating Holland. The Republic succeeded in keeping contact with the outside world, despite the attempted Dutch blockade, and stories of Dutch ruthlessness and treachery reached the international press and media. For instance, when the Dutch unilaterally violated the 1946 Linggadjati Agreement, which had been arranged under British auspices and established a cease-fire, by launching a brutal surprise assault on Republican territory, Australia was one of the powers which protested to the United Nations Security Council. Great publicity was also given internationally to Dutch efforts to prevent medical supplies reaching the Republican areas (which were mainly in Java and Sumatra). Again, it was the Dutch who unilaterally violated the 1948 Renville Agreement, reached under UN good offices, by delivering an all-out attack with heavy air support on the Republic. In this so-called 'police action', the Dutch captured Sukarno and Hatta, whom they again interned.

Guerrilla warfare continued unabated, however, and in the course of it Western plantations and other enterprises sustained great damage. The United States, as an importer of tin, rubber and oil, had great economic and strategic interest in Indonesia, and anticipated advantageous commercial relations with the new Republic once the Dutch had gone. Great pressure was, therefore, applied by the Americans to the Dutch government—including the threat to withdraw Marshall Aid—and finally, at the end of 1949, negotiations for the transfer of sovereignty were entered into by Holland, the Republic, and the various Dutch puppet states that had been created in the post-war period in the outer islands. The result was a constitution for a 'Republic of the United States of Indonesia' (RUSI), to which sovereignty over the whole territory of the former Netherlands East Indies was passed 'unconditionally and irrevocably' on 27 December 1949.

3

PERFORMANCE AND POTENTIAL

WESTERN writers often contrast the great potential wealth of Indonesia with its actual state of poverty. It is commonly implied that Indonesia's rulers are wholly to blame for this discrepancy. While it is of course true that their deficiencies have contributed to the situation, objective circumstances largely beyond their control can be shown also to have exercised a powerful influence.

In considering this, it is convenient to use the categories of land, labour, and capital. Land includes the fertility of the soil, the contents of the sub-soil, and the wealth of the surrounding seas. A noted geographer recently wrote that there was no reason to suppose Japanese soils to be inherently more productive than those of Java, and that therefore the explanation for the contrasting levels of productivity today must be sought in the higher level of technical efficiency of Japanese agriculture and, above all, in the much heavier use of fertilizer. Japan was never, of course, colonized while Java was, and that is the crucial historical distinction. The implication of the above for the future, however, is that with a technical transformation of Javanese (and Indonesian) agriculture along Japanese lines, a much greater population than at present could be fed at much more satisfactory levels, in terms of per capita intake of cereals. Nor is there anything intrinsically inadequate about the supply of essential dietary supplements—fruit, vegetables, fish, and eggs—though meat and dairy products will obviously for the foreseeable future have to be imported from neighbouring surplus areas, such as Australia and New Zealand, and paid for by exports.

The technical transformation of Indonesian agriculture demands industrialization. In turn, this rests on the supply of appropriate minerals such as iron and coal. Japan has had to import the necessary minerals. In contrast, Indonesia would appear to have adequate domestic supplies. Many parts of the archipelago have never been subjected to thorough survey. In other areas there are known to be extensive reserves of valuable minerals, but the necessary facilities for extraction, such as roads and railways, do not yet exist. The example of China is apposite. Before the revolution China imported the oil extracted from their colonies by the Western powers, and it was generally asserted that China lacked domestic reserves of this and other vital minerals. It is now known, following careful surveying since 1949, that China is one of the world's leading powers in terms of mineral resources—and is self-sufficient in the oil she was once forced to import. Natural resources, in practice, are *cultural appraisals*; given the appropriate sociocultural changes, the estimated wealth of a country, even in such apparently fixed and given quantities as mineral resources, can be constantly up-graded. Indonesia would seem in these terms to have exceptional promise for the future.

As far as labour is concerned, Indonesia has an abundance which, at present, is embarrassing. However, quantity is obviously not the only consideration: regard must be had to quality and to the availability of other factors of production (land and capital) as well. *Inherent* quality does not vary from one people to another—as the relevant UNESCO statement says '. . . given similar degrees of cultural opportunity to realize their potentialities, the average achievement of the members of each ethnic group is about the same'. On these grounds, we would expect Indonesia, with about twice Britain's population, to produce twice as many geniuses and twice as many Nobel Prize winners as Britain. But of course as between Britain and Indonesia there have not been 'similar degrees of cultural opportunity' in recent centuries. Indeed, the Dutch had one of the worst records among the colonial powers as educators. More than 90 per cent of the Indonesian people were illiterate at independence (compared with only 30 to 40 per cent in the neighbouring Philippines). A mere handful had completed anything that would be recognized as higher education. Since independence there has been a most thorough and sustained campaign to set this right. The young have been sent to school and college, while literacy has been carried to the villages by a variety of means. As a result, illiteracy has rapidly dwindled, while a growing proportion of the population have had higher education of one kind or another. (Indonesia —with the exception of West Irian—was in fact declared free from illiteracy at the end of 1964.) The consequences of this educational revolution could—and ought to—be incalculably beneficial to the country, only given the appropriate opportunities and incentives. Meanwhile, educational attainment has become *the* determinant of social status in contemporary Indonesia.

In passing it should be noted that health is a variable of great importance in any consideration of the quality of the labour force. Both mental and physical effort are impaired by many of the diseases and conditions associated with poverty.

It was one of the comforting myths of the colonial period that the 'native' population lacked ambition and the spirit of enterprise. Insofar as there was some truth in this, it could be ascribed to the factor alluded to above. But it never was really true. In Indonesian economic history there are numerous examples of local enterprise being thwarted by circumstances beyond the control of the ruled. Copra, for example, was pioneered by Indonesians. Smallholder rubber cultivators showed themselves remarkably responsive to shifts in market circumstances. But there was always the superior economic power of the Dutch and Chinese blocking the way to further advance. The economic problems of the post-1950 period are dealt with below, but for our purposes at the moment we may safely assume that there is no necessary bottleneck in enterprise or managerial skills to take into account in our survey of potential Indonesian wealth.

Which leaves us to consider capital. Indonesia is, of course, a poor country, and from that point of view chronically short of capital, which may be defined as the excess or surplus of economic resources over and above that portion required for immediate consumption. However, there are great inequalities in personal wealth, and the very existence of a privileged élite demonstrates that there *is* an economic surplus. In common with many developing countries, Indonesia has failed to harness this. Taxation has been relatively light, and in any case evaded. Nor have the wealthy in general used their resources productively, by investing it in new manufacturing enterprises, for example. They have preferred to indulge in conspicuous consumption or speculation—which, in the circumstances of Indonesia since independence, has offered satisfactory returns.

The mass of the population have, in contrast, had little to spare. But even with a population as poor as Indonesia's, capital can be raised for development purposes, as China has shown in the post-war period. The important thing is that the government must make sure that every increment in national wealth—however small—is accumulated and productively used, not dissipated. Moreover, the labour of the country, so often un- and under-employed, can itself be 'turned into capital' by direction into tasks requiring little but sweat and simple, available tools—tasks such as road building, improving irrigation systems, digging wells, and so on. By such methods Indonesia, like China, could set afoot a process of accelerating capital accumulation; so that, even in this category, the country is potentially wealthy. The role of overseas aid is discussed below, but it may be said here that Indonesia's experience since independence seems to afford confirmation of the thesis that the more 'aid' a country gets the poorer it becomes.

This brief examination serves to confirm Indonesia's great promise. It is now time to turn to the factors influencing her actual performance since the war.

We saw in the previous Chapter how independence was granted to a 'Republic of the United States of Indonesia' in 1949. The constitution of RUSI was federalist in character, and as it turned out, quite unworkable. Its defects were obvious. The state of Riau, with about 100,000 inhabitants, had the same Senate representation as the Republic of Indonesia, with 300 times the population. Nationalists saw it as an attempt by the Dutch to perpetuate their hegemony by classical colonial 'divide and rule' tactics, for several of the small component states had been carefully fostered by Holland. In a few months the federal system collapsed as member states one by one opted to merge with the Republic of Indonesia. A new, unitary, constitution was proclaimed on 17 August 1950, the fifth anniversary of the original proclamation of independence, and the country became simply the Republic of Indonesia.

A host of problems cried out for attention. The years of occupation and anti-colonial war had devastated the country. President Sukarno and Prime Minister Hatta faced many difficulties, not least of which was the shortage of trained and experienced people to assume responsibility for all the varied matters demanding action. In 1940, the last full normal year, only 240 Indonesians graduated from high school and 37 from college—out of an estimated population of 70.5 million. All in all, the number of people in 1950 (by which time the population had risen by about another 9 million) who had had genuinely higher education could be numbered only in hundreds. This incredibly small élite had to man the highest offices in the bureaucracy, the judiciary, the armed forces, the professions, and politics. Moreover, these men had been engaged for many years in activities other than those for which their training had prepared them.

Nor were the new Republic's difficulties with the Netherlands at an end. The 80,000 troops of the Dutch Royal Army (KL) were not immediately withdrawn, and in addition there were 65,000 Indonesian troops in the Royal Netherlands Indies Army (KNIL), some of them loyal to Holland. Units of these were involved in attempts at secession, assassination, and *coups d'état* in the early years of independence. The most stubborn resistance was met with in the South Moluccas, where an independent republic (the RMS—Republik Maluku Selatan) was proclaimed; guerrilla fighting here has persisted to the present, and a government in exile exists among the many South Moluccans who went to Holland with the Dutch after independence.

Then there were outstanding problems left unsolved or contentious by the agreements between Holland and Indonesia governing independence. One such was the future status of West Irian (West New Guinea). Despite Indonesian protests, the Dutch retained control over this area, although it had been an integral part of the Netherlands East Indies, and in this respect in no way differed from the rest of the archipelago. Contrary to undertakings given at the time of independence, the Dutch consistently refused to negotiate its future. It was this action, among others, which provoked Indonesia to dissolve the Commonwealth-type 'Union' with the Netherlands in 1954, to expel all remaining Dutch nationals and confiscate their property in 1957, and to sever diplomatic relations with Holland in 1960. Finally, in 1962, bowing to Indonesian diplomatic and military harrying tactics, and to international pressure, the Dutch agreed to transfer West Irian to Indonesia, with a face-saving provision for a self-determination referendum of the people there in 1969.

Another bone of contention was the very heavy debts with which Holland saddled the new state on independence, including the costs which the Dutch had incurred in their efforts to crush the Republic of Indonesia. This was only one of a number of economic grievances which marred the relationships of the former colony and its metropole. The Dutch sought to retain a major privileged position in the Indonesian economy, much as America had succeeded in doing after giving independence to the Philippines. But by 1957 or so Dutch influence in Indonesia was less than that of any other colonial power with any of its ex-colonies. It was not until 1963 that the first tentative diplomatic and trade links were re-established between Holland and Indonesia.

The Constitution and political system with which Indonesia embarked in 1950 were based upon Western models. In assessing their failure it is very important to bear in mind both the inadequacy of the preparation for responsible government afforded the Indonesians by the Dutch during the colonial period, and the very short period of time that has passed since independence. Since the Dutch had no real intention of quitting Indonesia, they never attempted the kind of provision of limited responsible government for the local people such as had characterized British rule in India and Burma. The Volksraad, as we have seen, remained in essentials a talking-shop.

But the time-scales involved are far more significant. The British constitution and political practices, to take one example, have been evolving in a context of relative political stability for several centuries. During this period Britain has never been colonized or occupied by a foreign power, and there has been a steady growth in and dispersal of national wealth, ensuring a notable degree of social consensus. Even so, it will be noted that it was not thought prudent to extend the franchise to all British adults until nearly a third of the way through the *present* century. Indonesia attempted to take the same step with her very first Electoral Law in 1953; indeed, she went further in that the vote was granted at 18 to men and women alike.

Furthermore, when we come on to talk about the political history of Indonesia in the post-independence period we would do well to keep in mind that even in the West the normal functioning of constitutional democracy is instantly suspended during periods of crisis (or 'crisis'). This is especially, but not solely, true of wartime. It was thought quite in order for General de Gaulle for example to take extraordinary steps to settle the political problems of France by assuming personal power when parliamentary democracy proved too unstable. President Sukarno, who was almost simultaneously introducing 'guided democracy' in conditions of much greater political instability and crisis in Indonesia, was very conscious of the double standard of morality applied by Western political and press commentators to his own and De Gaulle's actions.

Indonesia's experiment in constitutional democracy, the period of 'liberal democracy' as it is known, lasted only from December 1949 to the later years of the nineteen-fifties when 'guided democracy' took over, the transformation variously dated somewhere between 1956 and 1959. The minimal prerequisites for the successful functioning of constitutional democracy were really missing. At the outset, the genuine liberal commitment of a handful of the educated élite, backed up by a certain enthusiasm for the idea of democracy (rather vaguely conceived) in a wider circle, served to obscure this reality. President Sukarno, however, was already talking in 1949 of 'Eastern democracy . . . Indonesian democracy . . . a democracy with leadership'.

In what respects were the minimal prerequisites lacking? First, the indigenous middle-class was tiny. The commercial-economic bourgeoisie was mainly European or Chinese, and even if one were to stretch the term 'middle-class' to include all the literate Indonesians their numbers were still, at that time, relatively speaking small. Second, there was no significant bank of experience in the mechanics of operating a democracy of the Western kind. It is true that, by and large, the general election of 1955 went very well, 80 per cent of the eligible voters exercising their privilege, but there had been a prolonged build-up to this event for some years throughout the nation, almost every possible national and local occasion being converted to the purposes of electioneering. Moreover, voting in the villages was influenced— aside from outright intimidation and bribery—by considerations of social solidarity and traditional loyalties rather than by consideration of the relative merits of the programmes advanced by the respective parties. On top of that, during the course of the long three-year campaign, deep-rooted religious issues became inextricably confused with the more superficial political so that there was tense Muslim/anti-Muslim feeling, which for many outweighed all other considerations. Traditional Indonesian decision-making has been, not by voting and '50 per cent plus one' democracy, but by *musjawarah* (deliberation, discussion) and *mufakat* (agreement after deliberation); decisions are reached, not through majority, but by final arrival at the general will, the greatest attainable degree of consensus. In contrast, everybody in Britain, from school onwards, is familiar with, and personally acquainted with, all the business of elections, both to select representatives and to reach decisions.

Third, in surveying these minimal prerequisites, something must be said about national consensus. We have seen that geography and historical experience have militated against achievement of such a consensus in Indonesia. The national revolution for liberation from the Dutch papered over many of the cracks (although one recalls the 1948 uprising of the communists against the embattled Republic), but the early years of independence brought them all to light again, interfering with the unity of almost every national body. The principle polarities were these: *santri* and *abangan*; Javanese and non-Javanese; élites and masses; urbanites and peasantry; Java and the other islands; and what one political scientist has called 'administrators' and 'solidarity-makers' (that is, basically, those who put administrative efficiency as top priority contrasted with those who felt that, as against all those divisive impulses, what was principally required was a national ideology and national symbols powerful enough to rally all forces in Indonesia to one banner).

Santri/abangan as a dichotomy has, as we have seen, deep roots in Indonesian history, the one with business-commercial-religious functionary leadership, the other with *prijaji*-bureaucratic leadership. There was (and is) a tendency for the other polarities to fit into some kind of rough alignment with this basic one. For example, many of those to whom we have referred as the 'administrators' were men from the other islands in the *santri* tradition, while, conversely, many of the 'solidarity-makers' were Javanese in the *prijaji* tradition. Islam, of course, played a prominent part in these tensions; Sukarno's *Pantja Sila*, designed as a compromise statement of national purpose, never really satisfied the devout Muslims, and became, in fact and in time, associated with an anti-Muslim position.

The result was that there was no national class or group upon which to rest political stability. Even the armed forces (often a source of strength in new Afro-Asian states) were, at this stage, divided, for some elements of the old KNIL had to be absorbed among their old enemies the nationalist guerrillas. (There were also 'free enterprise' army units still at large, such as those associated with *Darul Islam*, the fanatical Islamic organization, in West Java.) Nor—hardly surprisingly in the circumstances—did any one of the proliferating political parties succeed in becoming a national party with majority support. Before the elections of 1955, no party ever held more than 52 seats in a Chamber of Representatives of 236; after the elections, no party held more than 57 seats out of 233. Furthermore, party discipline was weak. Between December 1949 and March 1957 no cabinet lasted longer than two years, and most considerably less. All were coalitions, both in the sense of being composed of members of various parties, and in the sense of being representative of a variety of cross-party interests.

It ought to be stressed, however, that whatever their other differences all the members of the active political élite *were* agreed on one thing—namely that the urban and rural poor should be prevented from converting their growing unrest into effective revolution. True social revolution would certainly deprive the élite of the new-found privileges which independence had brought. The tactic of the ambitious politician in this situation is clear: to incite and harness 'diversionary' political issues —language, religion, communalism—in order to obscure the underlying and really significant one—poverty and the relation between its persistence and the corruption and extravagance of the élite itself. In times of crisis, the welling revolutionary violence of the peasantry must similarly be found diversionary outlets—such as slaughtering each other in the name of religion, community, language group or some other ultimately irrelevant categorizing characteristic in order to prevent the poor uniting to turn upon their rich oppressors regardless of creed, ethnic roots or native tongue. (That peasant killed peasant, under the supervision of the armed forces, in the winter of 1965-66 in Indonesia affords a classic case of 'diversionary violence' in action.)

At first two parties—Masjumi and a reconstituted Indonesian Nationalist Party (PNI)—dominated, with the small Indonesian Socialist Party (PSI) influential because of the high calibre of its leaders. Apart from the continuation of revolts and regional separatist movements, things went on the whole fairly well, largely because the Korean War boosted the prices of Indonesia's principle primary product exports skyhigh. Foreign policy was neutralist with (compared with later periods) a slight pro-Western leaning.

About 1953 new alignments began to appear. The PKI, under the leadership of the young and able Aidit, staged a noticeable recovery, to become a significant factor in national politics. A section of Masjumi split away to form a new party, *Nahdatul Ulama* (Muslim Scholars) based largely in East Java. This seriously weakened Masjumi's national appeal, for its remaining support lay mostly in the outer islands. The new coalitions were based upon the PNI, Nahdatul Ulama, and a number of minor nationalist parties, with PKI support. Foreign policy swung to the left, and it was during this period that the historic conference of Afro-Asian nations was held at Bandung in Indonesia (1955), China and India both participating. Relations with Russia and

China improved, and the campaign to incorporate West Irian in Indonesia was launched.

The elections of 1955, so eagerly anticipated as some kind of panacea for all national ills—and especially for the instability, inefficiency, and growing corruption of parliamentary and party politics—failed completely to achieve their object. Four main parties emerged—the PNI, Masjumi, Nahdatul Ulama, and the PKI. The success of the last two (18.4 and 16.4 per cent of the popular vote respectively) and the virtual elimination of the PSI were the most noteworthy features of the results. There was no alternative but to try again to govern by coalition —in rapidly deteriorating objective circumstances precipitated by external as well as internal factors (the prices of Indonesia's exports were falling steeply from 1952 to 1959 while the prices of her imports were rising, for instance). But the parties continued to show themselves incapable of constructive co-operation, and—outside the PKI—incapable even of sustaining internal cohesion.

It was in these unpropitious circumstances that President Sukarno raised the question of 'guided democracy', articulating the rising national discontent at the performance of 'liberal' or 'Western' democracy. His own position under the 1950 constitution was unsatisfying to one of his energy and personal national stature; in theory he was a 'constitutional monarch', but in practice he played politics, having an especially close relationship with the PNI, but increasingly relying upon the PKI to counteract the authority and power of the army, whose prestige had grown with successes against regional rebels, and whose coherence had developed with time. Many army leaders were also critics of the party system; there is no Opposition in an army.

Vice-President Hatta, leading representative of the 'administrators' and a Sumatran by birth, resigned in 1956 in opposition to the drift of Sukarno's policies. In

1957 the President made public in greater detail his proposals. Their essence was that the cabinet should represent a broad cross-section of the parties, including the communists, and that it should work with a National Council which would include key ministers and representatives of various interest groups in Indonesian society (trade unions, youth movements, women, the armed forces, etc.). To these proposals there was prompt resistance, and a state of War and Siege had to be declared later in the year. In 1958 a major rebellion flared in Sumatra, which many distinguished Indonesians supported. But the armed forces as a whole remained loyal, and the revolt was readily suppressed.

It was at this time that continuing neo-colonial interference in Indonesia's internal affairs came most strikingly to light, since the Sumatran rebels were supplied from British and American bases in Malaysia and the Philippines while American pilots in American war planes flew missions for them. A joint U.S.-British invasion of Sumatra 'to protect the lives and properties of American and British nationals' (i.e. to protect the supply of Sumatran rubber, copra, oil and other important products) was contemplated. It was not hard to see the reasoning behind this intervention, because the PKI was gathering strength rapidly. In the 1957 provincial elections it markedly increased its share of the vote as compared with 1955, and its membership soared. Moreover, it controlled many other organizations such as SOBSI—the trade union federation—and the BTI or Peasant Front of Indonesia. And, under Aidit, its policy was one of support for Sukarno, a support he welcomed and indeed rewarded (for example, by defending the PKI from army suppression). With the defeat of the Sumatran revolt, American policy switched to support for some of the most staunchly anti-communist officers in the upper echelons of the army.

Despite these various pressures, Sukarno successfully steered his own course, restoring the Presidential-type constitution of 1945 in July 1959, and appointing a so-called *gotong rojong* parliament in the following March, at which time he himself became Prime Minister as well as President. His principal concern was to weld Indonesia into a nation lest the obvious social divisions tore it apart. For this reason, he placed strong emphasis upon Indonesia's place in the world. Large and impressive embassies were maintained abroad, and Djakarta became one of Asia's liveliest diplomatic capitals. Indonesian troops served in the UN's Congo operations. Sukarno himself undertook innumerable overseas trips; and because of the strategic and economic importance of his non-aligned country he was welcome in both communist and Western capitals as well as elsewhere in the Afro-Asian-Latin American world. A large press corps was resident in Djakarta; until December 1965 the Afro-Asian Journalists Association had its secretariat there.

It was also important for Sukarno to have nationalist causes capable of rousing popular feeling. One such was the long campaign to incorporate West Irian into Indonesia (where, indeed, it rightly and properly belonged in accordance with the well-established convention of international law that when a colony is granted independence the new sovereign independent power is entitled to the same boundaries as the colony it replaces). This campaign appealed both to the army, who saw in it another reason for maintaining its bloated establishment of 290,000 men (there was, in addition, a navy of 26,000 and an air force of 20,000), and the PKI for whom it was a stark anti-imperialist issue.

'Confrontation' with Malaysia, launched with the new

---

7. Ex-President Sukarno, who dominated the first twenty years of country's independence, on a visit to Egypt, with President Nasser.

Federation in late 1963, was in intention another 'national' policy, one behind which many forces in Indonesian society could range themselves. Historically, major political units in the region tended to incorporate parts of both Malaysia and Indonesia, as they now are. The present borders were only very recently decided upon—as a matter of colonial convenience—by the British and the Dutch. During the Second World War, Indonesian nationalist leaders in fact approached leading Malay figures and suggested a joint movement for independence, a suggestion which was rejected. The Malay leadership was at once more conservative than the Indonesian and at the same time suspicious of long-term Indonesian ambitions for the region.

After both Malaya and Indonesia had gained independence relations were proper rather than cordial, and subject to jolts from time to time—as, for example, when Indonesia accused Britain and Malaya of helping to supply and succour the 1958 Sumatra rebels. It was the project for a federation of Malaya with the remaining British dependencies in the area—the predominantly Chinese island of Singapore and the three Borneo territories (Sarawak, Brunei, and Sabah)—that resulted in the most serious strain. Indonesian leaders felt that something touching the interests of their country so intimately (Malaysian and Indonesian Borneo, for instance, would have a long common border) ought to have had their prior approval. In fact, discussions between representatives of the three countries most affected by the proposal—Malaya, Indonesia, and the Philip-

---

8. *Rivals for Power*
   (*a*) D. N. Aidit, former Secretary of the PKI (Communist Party of Indonesia), who was killed in the slaughter of communists which followed the 'September 30th Movement' coup of 1965.
   (*b*) General Suharto, President of Indonesia, the man who toppled Sukarno and crushed the Communist Party of Indonesia.

pines—almost reached agreement on matters of procedure and common interest. It appears now that British pressure on the Malayan leaders to go ahead as originally planned—and according to the Indonesians in violation of the key regional agreement (that reached at Manila in August 1963)—was an important factor in precipitating what President Sukarno called confrontation.

Predictably, the PKI whole-heartedly backed confrontation, branding Malaysia (the new federation) as a 'neo-colonialist creation', in view of the British role in its formation and the major British military and economic influence perpetuated by various provisions and agreements. Like Sukarno, the communists distrusted the purposes to which Western military bases in the region might be put. Both also resented the strongly pro-Western alignment of Malaysia's leaders. Sukarno for his part feared that the incorporation of Singapore's Chinese in Malaysia foreshadowed at some point in the future local Chinese domination of the neighbour he saw as part of the wider Malay world. The PKI on its side saw confrontation with Malaysia as one diversion from an awkward internal problem. Sukarno had brought several leading communists into positions of authority in his government bodies. They were thus identified to some extent with the fate of the government's economic policies, which were signally failing to alleviate the poverty of the people. Confrontation afforded the PKI a platform upon which their stance could be less ambiguous than it had to be on the poverty problem.

It might have been expected that the armed forces too would have welcomed confrontation, which offered to provide more chances for military glory. It is true that the nation's military leaders endorsed the anti-Malaysian campaign. But they also recognized professionally that Malaysia and the British were not West

Irian and the Dutch. Some of the anti-Malaysian operations mounted were conspicuously unsuccessful, albeit
limited in scope. Moreover, military aims and purposes
were inextricably intertwined with political: Malaysian
Chinese left-wingers and Malay supporters of Indonesia
were coming across into Indonesia for training and were
then being infiltrated back into Malaysia to undertake
subversion and political activity. Finally, when the bill
for confrontation began to come in, those in the Indonesian army who were not ideologically opposed to
Malaysia's neo-colonial pro-Western presence were readily persuaded that the cake was not worth the candle.
Apart from the mopping up of infiltrators landed on the
Malayan mainland by boat or parachuted in, the bulk
of the fighting took place in Borneo with its difficult
mountain, jungle, and swamp terrain. Large numbers of
British and Gurkha troops, with helicopters, were de-
ployed. In retaliation Indonesian crowds attacked British
properties, burning down the Embassy in Djakarta for
example, and in 1964 British businesses were expropriated.

In his concern for Indonesian national identity, Sukarno also elaborated a panoply of ideological symbols.
He sought to formulate his ideas in ways that could be
easily grasped and retained. An early attempt in this
direction was his statement of the *Pantja Sila* or five
basic state principles. Later appeared such exotics as
Manipol/USDEK and Nasakom at the time of transition to guided democracy (Manipol stood for the
Political Manifesto presented by Sukarno in his Independence Day Speech of 1959; USDEK is made up of the
initial letters of the five key phrases summing up the
contents of that speech; Nasakom is formed from the
front letters of *Nas*ionalisme, *A*gama, and *Kom*unisme
—that is nationalism, religion, and communism, the
coalition Sukarno sought to achieve). Neither these, nor

succeeding slogans had the content or power, however, to unite Indonesia effectively behind his policies.

Sukarno had been a prominent exponent of the concept of 'non-alignment' in international affairs. In common with many of the leaders of the new nations in Africa and Asia he had no wish to see his country embroiled in the Cold War between the Western powers and the Communist bloc. Sukarno at first sought to cultivate friendly relations with both protagonists (he delighted in being made welcome in all the world's major capitals), and in the 'fifties Indonesia's voting record in the UN reflected this desire, her vote splitting pretty evenly as between the blocs.

However, with characteristic shrewdness Sukarno was one of the first of the uncommitted statesmen to grasp the implications of the growing détente between America and Russia and of the ideological split between Russia and China. Increasingly he believed that world forces were split not three ways—capitalist, communist, non-aligned—but two—the 'old established forces' and the 'new emerging forces' (typically abbreviated to Oldefo and Nefo). These correspond broadly speaking with the white/coloured, rich/poor contrasts of which the world has become increasingly conscious as the gap between their standards of living has widened. Indonesia, of course, was firmly in the Nefo camp, the leadership of which Sukarno believed lay with China.

In the first half of the 'sixties, accordingly, Indonesia and China moved closer together diplomatically. (At the same time, Sukarno did not back-peddle on his policy of harassing and restricting the Chinese living in Indonesia; legislation sought to ban them from rural commerce and to preserve certain occupations and lines of business for Indonesians.) At the Belgrade Non-aligned Conference in 1961, Sukarno headed a 'left' bloc and Nehru a 'right' bloc. The Indonesian President argued that the eradication of all traces of colonialism and neo-colonialism was the first essential for world peace, while the Indian Premier gave first priority to suspension of nuclear tests and nuclear disarmament. The leftward movement of Indonesian foreign policy brought it increasingly into conflict with the Western powers, a fact that was mirrored in the UN. Finally, on 1 January 1965 Indonesia took the extraordinary and unprecedented step of leaving the United Nations (on Malaysia's election to the Security Council). Indonesia and China suggested that a rival international organization should be established for the 'new emerging forces'.

However prominent a part Indonesia played on the international stage, her domestic problems remained intractable. Concerning the facts there can be no dispute. An Indonesian newspaper editorial summed the economic situation up in the following words in November 1964: 'With the deplorable situation that we face today we are bound to get to the bottom much faster, and when we reach the bottom, things can't get any worse. From that point, the situation can only get better'. Chaerul Saleh, the then Minister for Basic Industries and Third Deputy Prime Minister, confessed in December of the same year that the first half of the vaunted 'Eight-year National Overall Development Plan 1961-69' had been a complete failure, and that it had not produced a single enterprise capable of earning desperately needed foreign exchange. The UN Food and Agricultural Organization reported that the most rapid inflation in the world in 1964 took place in Indonesia, yet things were even worse the following year, when rice prices in Djakarta rose by 660 per cent. Rubber exports, which account for about two-thirds of Indonesia's foreign exchange earnings, halved between 1961 and 1964. While the people were asked by Dr. Subandrio, the then Foreign Minister and Deputy Prime Minister, to hold back their desire for a better economic life in the interests of the Indonesian revolution, Sukarno went ahead with costly prestige projects such as a planetarium and a national theatre. Factories, lorries, ships, and mines stood idle because of shortages of spare parts and trained men. Corruption in state enterprises and the bureaucracy was described by the then Minister of Defence, General Nasution, as having reached 'fantastic proportions'.

Before passing summary judgement on Sukarno and his chief lieutenants, however, let us look at some of the limitations within which they were forced to work. When the national consensus, badly frayed though it had been before, finally broke in 1965, absolute tragedy overtook Indonesia. Sukarno had had some premonition of this from the start, and he therefore put the *political* task—the task of trying to forge national unity—first. It was a desperate race against deteriorating economic circumstances and he lost. But for twenty years he tried.

Of course there was corruption and conspicuous consumption. Sukarno's residences were fabulously furnished; his younger wives lacked for nothing; and when he travelled (which he did frequently) he took with him large and expensive entourages. Those in the élite with the capacity to do so emulated this ostentation. But we ought not to lose sight of our own recent past. Nineteenth-century Britain does not lack exemplars of luxurious living among the élites. Even Pitt the Younger, although possessed of few extravagant tastes except heavy drinking, went through an income of £10,000 a year (equivalent to at least £60,000 a year today) and left debts of £40,000. As for corruption, we perhaps tend to overlook how very recent is the British civil service's reputation for probity: it was during the course of the 19th century that the reforms necessary to produce an honest and efficient bureaucracy were undertaken, upwards of 150 years after our Revolution.

And if we are to blame Sukarno and his governments for the breakdown of 1965-66, we ought in fairness to recall the breakdown in the United States a century before—in much more propitious circumstances—in which over 600,000 persons died (about a fifth of the then population). Yet the USA as a young nation had every possible advantage as compared with Indonesia.

Finally, before looking at the staggering magnitude of the economic task which has so far defeated successive Indonesian administrations, let us not forget that, with all our wealth and opportunities, we in the West allowed poverty to linger on in the midst of growing plenty for far too long (and indeed still inexcusably do so). During the dark years of the Industrial Revolution in Britain when we were achieving 'take-off' into sustained economic growth—let us say the years 1780 to 1830—the standards of living of the mass of the people may well have actually deteriorated, and even a century later gross poverty persisted.

Yet we in the West had everything in our favour. Let us consider some of the advantages we enjoyed, and which, conversely, Indonesia and countries in her position lack. First of all, when we started to industrialize we had small populations. Britain in 1760 had about 8 million people, while the USA in 1780 had a mere 3 million. In contrast, the population of Indonesia is already past the 100 million mark. Second, Indonesian population is growing very much more rapidly than Western populations during their 'take-off'. The population of Western Europe and North America doubled between 1750 and 1850, but at current growth rates Indonesia's population could double every 30 years or less. Third, the starting densities of population are of different magnitudes. Western Europe's figure for the number of people per square kilometre in 1750 was about 23. Indonesia's today is 64, while that of Java is 477. Moreover, nearly 50 million Europeans emigrated to the almost empty countries of the Americas and Oceania between 1846 and 1930; no such population safety-valve exists for Indonesia's millions today.

Fourth, Indonesia today, in terms of measurable income per head of population, is very much poorer than were the presently developed countries when they embarked upon industrialization. We noted above that the Indonesian per capita annual income was estimated at £24 in 1962. In 1750, in contrast, the per capita income of England and Wales has been calculated at £70 per annum (in terms of today's prices). By 1962 this had jumped to well over £400. On the other hand, it is compatible with all the data we have to suggest that Indonesians were *better off* in 1850 than they were in 1950, and probably better off in 1750 than in 1850.

That the graphs of national income per capita should contrast so sharply is not, of course, coincidence. Which leads us to the fifth point. The West, in industrializing and embarking upon sustained economic growth, was faced with a world of markets to conquer, and was without powerfully entrenched competitors. Once control had been imposed over a major part of the globe in the form of colonies, the West was so able to arrange matters that advantage accrued to it cumulatively. But the reverse was true for the colonies such as Indonesia. Their position cumulatively deteriorated, certainly in relative terms. Now, trying to develop and industrialize in the face of the powerful disadvantages outlined above, countries such as Indonesia look out at a world the markets of which are already dominated by great and powerful industrial countries, which also exert controlling influence on world prices and most of the other circumstances relevant to the steady generation and accumulation of wealth.

The effective control over commodity prices exerted

by the countries that are her customers is especially serious for Indonesia (and countries like her) whose economy has become, as a result of colonialism, so dependent upon a handful of primary product exports. Over 70 per cent of export earnings derive from rubber, petroleum, and tin, all sensitive to demand and supply factors outside the control of the Indonesian rulers.

So, with all these handicaps and obstacles in mind, we ought not to judge too harshly the performance of the Indonesian economy since the war. Moreover, there *have* been real achievements. While many of the big show-piece projects have foundered, many smaller, and perhaps locally inspired, projects have made beneficial changes in the life of the people. Great leaps have been made in education, with the progressive conquest of illiteracy, and dedicated workers in the field of public health have reduced the incidence of many former scourges. The revolution and Indonesia's new place in the world have made her people development-conscious as never before. The pressure of this consciousness, the aspiration for those standards of life familiar from the cinema and illustrated magazines, is a factor Indonesia's rulers will never be able to ignore.

To point out the enormous adverse circumstances militating against Indonesia's attempts to develop economically is in no way to excuse or condone the dereliction of those guilty of gross corruption and dissipation and of selfishness. But these sins become manifest within a social context. It is not a question of inherent racial weakness or incapacity. The China that produced Chiang Kai-shek's warlords also produced Mao Tse-tung's Liberation Army. If Sukarno cannot be the Mao of Indonesia, he would certainly rather be remembered as the Sun Yat-sen than as the Chiang Kai-shek—that is, be remembered as the man who gave his country its sense of nationhood.

4

TODAY AND TOMORROW

INDONESIA'S 'today' dawned in the first few days of October 1965. Changes so profound took place then and thereafter in the Indonesian leadership and the country's policies that a new chapter is entirely in order.

Confrontation with Malaysia exacerbated Indonesia's economic problems and contributed nothing to the solution of her political problems—on the contrary. Aside from the direct costs incurred through troop movements, armed sorties into Malaysian Borneo, and similar contingencies, there were indirect costs. Trade between Indonesia and Malaysia was officially banned. This was a serious step, because Singapore had handled a large part of Indonesia's trade. It is true that it inflicted economic damage upon Malaysia too, but the loss was greater for Indonesia. Similarly, although the Malaysian government had to increase its defence spending (and cut down on economic development), it was helped substantially by Britain, Australia, and New Zealand, both in money and troops.

Although at first there appeared to be a substantial degree of national agreement on Sukarno's policy of 'crush Malaysia', the added difficulties which it brought in its wake, on top of the already steadily deteriorating economic position, produced opposition. Smallholders in the outer islands especially resented the ban on trade with Singapore and other neighbouring ports, for there was good money to be earned there instead of the Indonesian rupiah, which had been devalued several times since independence but always remained worth much less than the official rate indicated. President Sukarno tried to persuade the smallholders to sell their commercial produce through official channels and through named Indonesian ports.

In addition to their economic grievances, Sumatrans were conscious of their ties with Malaya. Many Malays were immigrants or descendants of immigrants from Sumatra. There has been sporadic talk on both sides of the Malacca straits since the war of the possibility of Sumatra and Malaya forming a political unit with, for some people, much to commend it; many Achinese are said to favour the idea.

While there were those in the armed forces who wished vigorously to press ahead with confrontation, others entertained serious and growing doubts about the wisdom of the policy. There were differences between branches of the armed forces, and differences between senior officers and junior. The senior ranks of the army itself contained a majority of conservative and implacably anti-communist figures, men with whom the United States government, through all the vicissitudes of official American-Indonesian relations (all US aid to Indonesia was suspended during the height of confrontation), kept contact. It was in these and allied circles in the bureaucracy and elsewhere among the élite that alarm was being felt at the growing connection between Indonesia and China, with consequent international isolation, and at the growth of the PKI and its front organizations (it claimed 3 million members in 1963, and a further 14 million supporters of women's, youth, peasants', and other related movements).

Ever since the promulgation of guided democracy and the crushing of the Sumatra revolt of 1958, the army had been strengthening its position and power. It had a growing influence at all levels of administration. Army men figured prominently in Sukarno's cabinets and other representative and governmental bodies. In the regions the local army commanders wielded great, and sometimes almost autonomous, authority. Expropriated foreign undertakings were in their hands. Russia and the other East European countries on the one hand, and the United States on the other, granted vast credits for the purchase of military equipment of all kinds and for training in their use.

The parties, on the other hand, had in general fared badly. Masjumi and the PSI were banned in August 1960, partly because some of their leaders had been involved in the 1958 revolt. The others who wished to survive had to accept Sukarno's *Pantja Sila* and other ideological pronouncements, and to help propagate them. Ten, including the PKI, accepted these conditions, but their freedom of manoeuvre was closely circumscribed. One, Partai Murba, was subsequently banned.

Sukarno was well aware of his exposed position in relation to the army. Although he had always been able at moments of crisis to rally the people to his own person—to many he was the living symbol of Indonesian nationhood, and his charismatic oratory had always hitherto proved highly effective—independence had failed to bring to the masses the benefits that had been promised of it, and disillusion was rampant. In an attempt to unite all the parties as a counterpoise to the army, Sukarno set up a National Front in 1960 but it foundered. In these circumstances, the *logic* of his position dictated growing links with the PKI, far and away the largest of the parties and the one possessed of the strongest and most coherent organization, apart altogether from any developing convergence of ideological positions.

Similarly, it was in the nature of the army leadership's position that it would seek to rally all anti-communist forces in Indonesia. It was for this reason that those who had joined the 1958 rebellion and were still holding out in Sumatra and Sulawesi were offered generous terms to 'return to the fold of the Republic' in 1961. The leaders and 100,000 men accepted the offer. The following year the leader of the Darul Islam rebels in West Java was captured, whereupon his followers surrendered. The leniency with which these—and other, minor—anti-communist rebels were treated on 'returning to the fold' was in marked and significant contrast to the bloodbath which accompanied suppression of the communist rising of 1948 and was to accompany the anti-communist terror of 1965-66.

This process of polarization was not, of course, unrelated to underlying and deep social forces at work in Indonesia. Observers noted many cross-currents. Some thought the primary tension was that between the Javanese and the non-Javanese. They could point to much evidence. The Javanese Sukarno, for instance, derived his main support from the three parties with their roots in Java (the PKI, Nahdatul Ulama, and the PNI) while he had banned the two principle parties of the outer islands (the PSI and Masjumi). In contrast, army chief General Nasution was Sumatran. Again, one of the main bones of contention in the country was that the outer islands earned the bulk of the foreign exchange while the problems of overcrowded Java dictated that the major part of the government's development expenditure be concentrated there. Other commentators drew attention to rising tension between those in the *santri* and those in the *abangan-prijaji* traditions respectively, in which clash the role of Islam in the state was a central issue.

It would be undesirable to over-simplify a complex situation, but it seems that basically the polarization of which we have spoken had class roots. Such an analysis can be reconciled with the data. First, it is not hard to see why the progressive and anti-imperialist parties had their main strength in Java (the PKI, the PNI, and Nahdatul Ulama—the latter anti-imperialist because anti-Christian and anti-Western). Java's experience of colonialism had been the longest and most traumatic, and the damage her indigenous social system had undergone the most severe. In contrast, the outer islands in general had had a relatively brief exposure to colonialism—and with certain off-sets for the local people in the form of opportunity to share in the profits of expanding commercial markets as smallholders.

Moreover, rural impoverishment, largely as a result of prolonged colonialism, had gone much further on Java than elsewhere. Despite paper 'rural reforms', successive post-independence governments had signally failed to arrest the process. Fragmentation of holdings as a result of population growth in areas of high initial densities was a powerful agent making for inequality. There would come a time when the individual plots of the poorer peasants were too small to be viable, whereupon they would be sold to richer peasants (or yielded up to creditors), while their former owners went to work for those with larger holdings. In this way, many of the poorer peasants sank to the status of landless labourer or share-cropper, while the richer ones were able to accumulate land into large holdings. Again, things were in general quite different on the outer islands where there was land to spare and where incomes could be earned from the sale of side crops. Broadly speaking, there developed a 'proletarianized' peasantry on Java and a 'bourgeoisified' peasantry on the outer islands. In the first case, revolutionary attitudes were engendered among the poor peasants by contact with oppressive landlords, extortionate money-lenders and small tradesmen, corrupt and haughty bureaucrats and soldiers locally, and with others able to inflict harm and humiliation. In the other case, appropriate attitudes favoured minimum government interference (i.e. free enterprise as opposed to the socialism proposed by the leaders of the left-wing peasantry in Java as a solution to their problems) and maximum contact with the international economy, particularly that major portion of it dominated by the rich Western powers.

Nor does a class analysis preclude taking cognizance of the important *santri-abangan* dichotomy. Frequently those middle peasants in Java who prospered at the expense of their neighbours were *santri*, motivated by calvinistic principles of the 'work hard-pray hard' kind. Many of the money-lenders and small traders were *santri*. On the other hand, it was easy for those anxious to fulfil their social obligations in accordance with traditional Javanese *abangan* values to incur debt. Class conflict, that is, was exacerbated by an historically deeply seated cultural split. On the outer islands where Islam was strong it was frequently directed against Javanese labourers.

The implications of this polarization were not lost on Sukarno and those about him. But the more Sukarno tried to integrate the communists into the establishment, the more he alarmed the conservatives. Confrontation, designed to align both armed forces and communists, was narrowing down international support. The Western powers, from whom massive aid had been forthcoming in the past, had withdrawn financial support, while relations with Russia and East Europe had been strained since the autumn of 1962 or thereabouts (as a result of Indonesian friendship with China and delays in paying interest and instalments on Russian loans). Without outside aid and foreign private investment—and withdrawal of American approval automatically ruled Indonesia beyond the pale as far as the international economic bodies (World Bank, International Monetary Fund, etc.) were concerned—the only realistic alternative strategy for development was that derived from the Chinese experience. But this would involve expropriating landlords, removing the privileges of the élite, uprooting corruption, and in general precipitating the social confrontation and show-down it had been the prime object of Sukarno's policies to avoid.

Obviously, the uneasy truce could not last. Sukarno's health was suspect, and every report or rumour of illness provoked a welter of speculation and a wave of uncertainty. The PKI, acutely conscious of the gap in firepower between their own cadres and the army, early in 1965 called upon the President to arm the people 'in defence of the revolution'. This Sukarno, limited by the power of the army, could not do. As the year wore on, tension mounted. The storm broke on the evening of 30 September.

Units of President Sukarno's palace guard, led by Lieutenant-Colonel Untung, seized a number of strategic points in Djakarta, including the broadcasting station, and announced the formation of an 'Indonesian Revolutionary Council' by a movement styling itself the 'September 30 Movement'. Six top right-wing army generals were captured and murdered (but two of the most important—Nasution and Suharto—escaped). President Sukarno left Djakarta for Halim Air Base, ostensibly to be within reach of a plane in case of emergencies; but it was here that communist youth groups had received military training from the pro-communist Indonesian air force.

However, regular army units had been converging on Djakarta for celebration of Armed Forces Day (5 October), and the revolt was quickly broken, the strategic points in the capital being re-taken during the course of 1 October. Resistance to the army continued in the countryside, especially of East and Central Java (the traditional Javanese *abangan* heartlands), and indeed continues, but the counter-coup was crushingly effective.

Sukarno, bowing to necessity and striving still to save something from his collapsing policies, quickly reasserted his primacy, while delegating to General Suharto the task of 'restoring peace'. Despite the President's attempts to protect leading communists and pro-communists, and to restrain the army and activist Muslim organizations, this 'restoring of peace' took the form of an unprecedented human slaughter. Throughout the archipelago PKI members and sympathisers, and their wives and children, were rounded up and put to death. Estimates of the number of victims vary—and it will never be possible to be exact—but certainly several hundred thousand people were thus executed summarily, and perhaps as many as a million. Having thus, for the time being, eliminated the PKI as an organized force in Indonesian politics, the army sought to legitimize its authority by bringing to trial, on the charge of complicity in the alleged Untung-PKI coup, a number of prominent figures of the old order—including Dr. Subandrio (sentenced to death), Commander of the Air Force Omar Dani (sentenced to death), and others, among them key figures of the PKI. Aidit himself was captured and killed. (Untung was subsequently shot in a military prison.)

In February 1967 Sukarno transferred all executive power to Suharto, and in the following month Suharto was appointed Acting President while the Provisional People's Consultative Congress at the same time stripped Sukarno of all governmental powers. So ended the reign of Indonesia's first President, and one of the post-war world's most supple and enduring political leaders.

These events are too near for adequate assessment and judgement to be made. The available evidence can be so used to support conflicting interpretations. All that can be done here is to point to certain salient features.

The army case is that the PKI planned the coup. This it is said to have done in conjunction with sympathisers in the armed forces—especially in the air force and the marines (KKO)—and with the full knowledge of such politicians as Dr. Subandrio, and the encouragement and incitement of Peking's communist leaders. Evidence in favour of this view consists of 'confessions' (some subsequently retracted and blamed on torture) of captured communists, the names of the members of Untung's 'Revolutionary Council' (certain leading communists, Dr. Subandrio, Omar Dani, and others), and the known contacts between some of the accused and China about this time.

On the other hand, there appear to be several inexplicable features of the coup and counter-coup if this is the whole story. Why, for example, did the PKI, faced with the fact of Untung's original coup, adopt the line that this was an internal army affair? At no time were communist and front organizations called on to the streets in support; indeed what surprised those eye witnesses who chanced to be in the country at the time was the ease with which the PKI supporters were rounded up and killed or imprisoned. *After a time* organized left-wing resistance arose, but surely a party that had planned to take power would have planned rather more than the seizure of a broadcasting station? Moreover, it is the movement of army units in the days before the fateful 30 September that are surely suspicious—forestalling altogether too neatly to be fortuitous what were to emerge as the army's needs.

The PKI case is, in fact, that the army, under the leadership of a right-wing 'Council of Generals', financed and supported by the American CIA (Central Intelligence Agency), had for long been planning to seize power—perhaps on 5 October—to reverse the leftwards direction of Indonesia's policies. When news of this leaked, short-notice action by left-wing junior army officers and units sympathetic to Sukarno had to be hastily mounted. This afforded the army leaders the perfect justification for the mass murders that followed. The PKI support their version of events by charging that the American Seventh Fleet was in Indonesian waters at the crucial period. It is also alleged that the army moved so swiftly throughout the archipelago to round up communists and supervise their 'elimination', that the operation can only have been one long contemplated and planned.

Whatever the truth, the immediate results were these. First, after negotiations, confrontation with Malaysia was officially brought to an end in the summer of 1966. (Ironically, Malaysia as originally planned broke up with the secession of Singapore in August 1965). Subsequently, early in August 1967, Indonesia joined Malaysia, Singapore, Thailand, and the Philippines in forming the Association of South-East Asia States (Asean); later in the month Indonesia and Malaysia formally restored full diplomatic relations. Second, the new Indonesian leaders contacted the Western powers and arranged with a consortium of creditors for immediate emergency financial aid. In return, the industrial nations concerned were granted certain important economic concessions in Indonesia. These included the return of assets expropriated by Sukarno; the unfreezing of profits and dividends long frozen by Indonesia; the passing of a new investment law encouraging foreign investment by the granting of real advantages (tax holidays, guaranteed repatriation of profits and dividends, safeguards against nationalization, tariff protection, etc.); and deflationary measures aimed at establishing a favourable 'climate' for foreign investment.

Despite the generally enthusiastic welcome extended to the Indonesian *orde baru* (new order) in the West, the achievement has not been unmixed. Persecution not only of communist suspects but also of local Chinese was greatly stepped up. Rich Chinese fled the country in great numbers. Poor ones were in some areas (for instance Atjeh) rounded up in port areas and invited to leave by whatever means they might devise. This was a reflection of the Malay-racist and Islamic slant of the right-wing generals' main social support (fear of the Chinese was a strong common bond drawing the right-wing Malaysian Malay leadership and the *orde baru* leaders of Indonesia together). At the same time it is interesting that Suharto's government has chosen to forge links with Chiang Kai-shek, the anti-communist Chinese leader supported by the Americans on the island of Formosa. The numbers of political prisoners in Indonesia's jails has risen steeply, and some of those previously held by Sukarno have been taken from their cells and shot out of hand (for example, Dr. Soumokil, President of the self-styled Republic of the South Moluccas, on 12 April 1966). Possession of the works of Mao Tse-tung has become an offence, punishable by imprisonment.

Assessments of prospects for the future must necessarily be speculative. But perhaps some guidance is to be sought in the experience of neighbouring countries which have chosen a similar course. The line-up of the new Association of South-East Asian States is highly significant, bringing together as it does those countries in the region most closely identified with the Western cause. The Philippines has important American military bases, and has long rested its economic development on encouragement of private, including foreign, investment. Thailand similarly holds major US bases (from which Vietnam is bombed), and relies for economic growth on domestic and foreign capitalism. Malaysia retains British bases, affords facilities to the Americans fighting in Vietnam, and again has taken the free enterprise path to growth.

Since Indonesia's change of leaders, the pattern of her external and internal policies has assimilated itself increasingly to this model. Large numbers of American military 'advisers' have appeared in Indonesia to help modernize the armed forces, while the US government has invested billions of dollars in the improvement of existing military bases and the construction of nearly a dozen new ones. In this way, an important gap in the chain of Western bases 'containing' China has been conveniently plugged. A crescent of countries with anti-communist and anti-Chinese governments now swings through South-East Asia, commanding it strategically and encompassing a variety of resources of vital concern to the West in general and the United States in particular (tin, rubber, manganese, oil, etc.)

It is true that economic aid and foreign investment will be attracted to Indonesia by the policies of her present rulers. The question is, however, whether these will prove beneficial in the long run. Aid in its present form entails eventual burdens (in the form of interest payments and repayments), and experience has shown that dependence upon it tends to become progressive—borrowing more to service previous loans—which gives tremendous power to the rich lending countries or agencies (the Indian case is relevant here). Moreover, aid which finds its way through a variety of channels to the pockets of the élite tends to be dissipated in balance of payments-straining purchases of imported luxury goods. China, whose progress in raising worker and peasant living standards had so impressed Sukarno and his closest political associates, has, on the other hand, achieved what she has totally without outside economic assistance since 1960.

Then again, those countries in the region which have enjoyed significant private foreign investment are by no means unambiguous economic success stories. Certainly, urban industrial enclaves are conjured into existence, but the amount of employment they offer locally is very restricted, and the benefits from their operation tend to be confined to the urban élite and to the Western investors. Rural living standards are typically hardly affected. Indeed, after six or seven decades of American investment, the Philippine islands have the poorest and most oppressed peasantry in South-East Asia (one might of course also refer here to the countries of Latin America—which, after *over a hundred years* of independence under right-wing, often military, leaders, with the main economic assets in the hands of United States investors, have nearly all failed to solve the problem of rural poverty). Rural living standards are also stagnant in Thailand and Malaysia. In all three countries such industrialization as has taken place has absorbed but a fraction of the growing unemployment caused by rising population.

In these circumstances, it is not difficult to see that sources of social conflict are bound to persist and intensify. Eventually the growing gap between rural living standards and the wealth of the élite is bound to precipitate conflict. Today there are peasant movements in the Philippines, north-east Thailand, and northern Malaysia dedicated to armed struggle. It is precisely in these circumstances that the presence of foreign troops is most dangerous; the élite may feel impelled to call upon those troops for assistance in putting down rural discontent, and the first steps along the road to another Vietnam will have been taken.

As far as Indonesia is concerned, the future is indeterminate. The crushing of the PKI may at the moment appear complete. But several members of the Central Committee of the Party escaped, and exile groups exist in Peking, India, Albania, and elsewhere. Moreover, armed resistance to the new leaders continues; in early 1968 it was reported to be stiffening. We would do well to recall, too, the comparable crushing of the Chinese Communist Party in 1927, when Chiang Kai-shek turned upon it and massacred thousands of its members. Yet within little more than twenty years the tables had been turned. There are indications that Sukarno's supporters have by no means disappeared or given up hope. A former Prime Minister of Indonesia, and a close associate of the former President, Ali Sastroamidjojo, was arrested in August 1967 and accused of complicity in a plot to restore Sukarno and Hatta to power.

The real test for Indonesia's leaders today is their readiness and ability to tackle rural poverty. To do so effectively, however, will call for unusual political courage, since it will involve drastically trimming the wealth and privileges of precisely those social groups that sustain the army in power. If nothing effective is contrived in this sector, rural unrest will persist, and become increasingly difficult to contain. The communists lurking in the countryside will certainly learn to work with and harness the discontents of the poor peasants, as their counterparts have so effectively done in South Vietnam.

As for the rapidly swelling urban conglomerations, their impoverished inhabitants constitute a volatile and unpredictable political element. In Indonesia, the true employed proletarian—the factory worker and skilled artisan—is a comparative rarity. It is the unemployed and casually employed—*lumpen* proletarians—who make up the urban mob. Their attachments are fickle— one day cheering Sukarno and burning down American property, the next hailing Suharto and destroying PKI headquarters. The army has so far used this element skilfully, but bread and circuses will be required to retain its allegiance.

The terrible events of the days and weeks following 1 October 1965 will not readily be forgotten. They cannot but have deepened already deep splits in Indonesian society. The surviving relatives of the victims will long nourish vengeance. Another dimension has been added to the long-standing *santri-abangan* duality, with all its over- and under-tones discussed above.

Finally, it remains to be seen whether the army leaders will show the same skill in using the symbols of nationalism, and the same shrewdness in manipulating foreign policy, as Sukarno did for so long. The encouragement to foreigners to come in and exploit Indonesia's most valuable resources (as in the colonial past) may well rebound. There has seemed an almost indecent haste to dispose of some assets to foreign buyers. Too intrusive an American presence would almost certainly arouse the same reaction of local resentment and resistance as it has done elsewhere in South-East Asia— including the Philippines, Thailand, and Malaysia. Moreover, in the long run Sukarno's policy of accommodation with China may appear as the more reasonable and sensible. American policy, under domestic and international pressure, may change, and the American presence in South-East Asia, at present so mighty, may overnight (in historical terms) disappear permanently from the region. But China cannot disappear, or be made to disappear. She must legitimately concern herself with overt threats to her security near her borders. American bases constitute one such threat. Countries harbouring them cannot expect to have harmonious relations with their giant neighbour. It is a matter seriously to be pondered.

SUGGESTIONS FOR FURTHER READING

FACTUAL

J. S. FURNIVALL, *Netherlands India* (Cambridge U. P., 1944). The standard socio-economic history.

S. SJAHRIR, *Out of Exile* (John Day, 1949). The journal kept by a leading Indonesian nationalist intellectual during his exile in the nineteen-thirties. The author was Indonesian Prime Minister 1945-47 and died in 1966.

G. McT. KAHIN, *Nationalism and Revolution in Indonesia* (Cornell University Press, 1952). An indispensable classic.

J. C. VAN LEUR, *Indonesian Trade and Society* (van Hoeve, 1955). One of the first challenges to the 'colonialist' view of Indonesian history by a European scholar.

W. F. WERTHEIM, *Indonesian Society in Transition* (van Hoeve, 1956). An original and suggestive analysis, methodically presented.

F. A. WAGNER, *The Art of Indonesia* (McGraw-Hill, 1959). Full coverage of the arts of the country.

SELOSOEMARDJAN, *Social Changes in Jogjakarta* (Cornell University Press, 1962). An unusually interesting, readable and informative study of social, economic and political change in the heartland of the Indonesian revolution. The author is an Indonesian scholar and administrator.

C. GEERTZ, *Agricultural Involution* (University of California Press, 1963). One of several books by an American anthropologist who has made contributions of outstanding originality to Indonesian studies.

RUTH T. McVEY (editor), *Indonesia* (Human Relations Area Files Press, 1963). An invaluable collection of authoritative essays. Extensive references and book lists.

J. D. LEGGE, *Indonesia* (Prentice-Hall, 1964). A thoughtful and balanced commentary on the history of Indonesia and on rival interpretations of that history.

J. M. PLUVIER, *Confrontations* (O.U.P., 1965). A short but concentrated and carefully reasoned analysis of Indonesian politics since 1919.

CLIVE DAY, *The Dutch in Java* (O.U.P., 1966). Reprint of a classic account, first published in 1904.

Reference should also be made to the following standard works:

C. A. FISHER, *South-East Asia—A Social, Economic, and Political Geography* (Methuen, 1964).

D. G. E. HALL, *A History of South-East Asia* (Macmillan, 2nd edition 1964).

G. McT. KAHIN (editor), *Major Governments of Asia* (Cornell University Press, 2nd edition 1963).

G. McT. KAHIN (editor), *Governments and Politics of South-East Asia* (Cornell University Press, 2nd edition 1964).

IMAGINATIVE AND TRAVEL

AHMED ALI (editor), *The Flaming Earth: Poems from Indonesia*. Translations of Indonesian poetry of the revolutionary period, including works by the most famous Indonesian poet Chairil Anwar.

JOSEPH CONRAD, *Almayer's Folly*. Brilliant novel set in the Indonesia of the colonial period.

E. DOUWES DEKKER (pseudonym 'Multatuli'), *Max Havelaar*. The famous exposé of Dutch oppression in Java. Innumerable editions in many languages, including English.

J. M. ECHOLS (editor), *Indonesian Writing in Translation*. A representative selection.

MOCHTAR LUBIS, *Twilight in Djakarta*. A novel of Djakarta's social and political life in the nineteen-fifties by an anti-Sukarno journalist.

B. RAFFEL (editor), *An Anthology of Modern Indonesian Poetry*. Represents all the major Indonesian poets.

M. H. SZEKELY-LULOFS, *Rubber*. A novel of plantation life in colonial Indonesia. The author had been a planter in Sumatra, and was unusually sympathetic to the Indonesian workers. Wrote a number of other novels with similar themes.

Two recent travel books are:

I. SOUTHALL, *Indonesia face to face* (1965).

M. WILLIAMS, *Five Journeys from Djakarta* (1966).

SOME DATES IN INDONESIAN HISTORY

c.3000 B.C. onwards Immigration of 'Malay' peoples into Indonesian archipelago from the north

c.1st to 2nd centuries A.D. onwards Indian Hindu and Buddhist immigration into Indonesia

2nd century Early diplomatic relations between China and Java mentioned in Chinese chronicles

413-414 Chinese Buddhist priest Fa Hsien visits Java, the first of several visiting Chinese and other foreign scholars in the following centuries

7th century onwards The Buddhist empire of Srivijaya, starting in Sumatra, spreads to most of what is today Indonesia

8th century onwards Construction of Borobudur and other famous monuments in Java

12th century onwards Islam establishes footholds in the archipelago

13th to 14th centuries Rise of the kingdom and empire of Madjapahit, based on Java and spreading to most of what is today Indonesia

1509 First entry of the Portuguese into Indonesia

1596 First Dutch expedition reaches Indonesia

1602 Foundation of *Vereenigde Oostindische Compagnie* (VOC—Dutch East India Company)

17th and 18th centuries Gradual extension of VOC trading monopoly and sovereignty in the archipelago

1799 End of Company rule in Indonesia

1811-1816 British rule Indonesia

1824 Treaty of London. British withdraw from remaining Indonesian possessions in return for Singapore

1825-30 The Java War; resistance led by Prince Diponegoro

1830 Introduction of the Culture System

1860 *Max Havelaar* published, critical of Culture System

1870   Agrarian and Sugar Laws effectively end the Culture System

1873-1903   The Atjeh War

1901   Dutch Queen announces inquiry into the 'diminishing welfare of the people of Java'

1908   Foundation of *Budi Utomo* (Noble Endeavour)—the pioneering Indonesian cultural-nationalist organization

1912   Foundation of *Sarekat Islam* and *Mohammadiah*

1918   Dutch institute a People's Council (Volksraad)

1920   Formation of Indonesian Communist Party (PKI)

1924   Formation of *Perhimpunan Indonesia* (Indonesian Students' Association)

1926-27   Revolution led by the PKI

1927   Formation of the PNI (Indonesian Nationalist Party)

1928   The Malay language adopted as the Indonesian national language

1930   Trial of Sukarno

1933   Revolt of the Indonesian crew of the Dutch warship 'De Zeven Provincien'

1942-5   Japanese occupation

1945   Indonesian independence proclaimed. British and Dutch troops land

1946   Linggadjati Agreement grants *de facto* Dutch recognition to the Republic of Indonesia in Java, Madura, and Sumatra. British troops leave

1947   Britain and the USA recognize Indonesia. First Dutch 'Police Action'

1948   PKI revolt in Madiun, East Java. Second 'Police Action'

1949   Round Table conference at The Hague, Holland, grants Indonesian independence

1950   'Republic of the United States of Indonesia' replaced by a unitary Republic of Indonesia

1952   Rising tension between Holland and Indonesia over West Irian

1953   ECAFE conference held in Bandung, Indonesia

1954   Dissolution of Indonesian-Dutch Union. Meeting of Colombo Power premiers at Bogor, Java

1955 Asian-African Conference at Bandung. Nationality Treaty concerning the Indonesian Chinese signed between China and Indonesia. First general elections

1956 Sukarno pays visits to many countries, including the big three (China, Russia, and America). Hatta retires from Vice-Presidency

1957 Dutch enterprises in Indonesia expropriated. Steps taken towards 'Guided Democracy'

1958 Large-scale rebellion in Sumatra and Celebes crushed by central government

1959 Return to Constitution of 1945, confirming Sukarno's primacy

1960 Appointed *gotong rojong* parliament replaces elected one, and Sukarno becomes Premier as well as President. Indonesia breaks off diplomatic relations with Holland over West Irian

1961 8-Year National Overall Economic Development Plan adopted. Agreement signed for massive military aid from Russia in the campaign to regain West Irian

1962 Agreement signed for re-incorporation of West Irian in Indonesia after American mediation between Holland and Indonesia. Revolt in Brunei against the Malaysia project supported by Indonesia.

1963 Manila Agreements between Indonesia, Malaya, and the Philippines. Subsequently Indonesia and the Philippines withhold diplomatic recognition from Malaysia and Indonesia launches 'Confrontation'

1964 Indonesia forging close relations with China. Indonesian infiltrators penetrate Malaysia in pursuit of Confrontation

1965 Indonesia leaves the United Nations when Malaysia is elected to the Security Council. Rising tension in Indonesia occasioned by economic hardship and the futility of Confrontation culminates in the 'September 30th Movement'—an attempted coup suppressed by the Army. Diplomatic relations reopened with the Netherlands

INDEX

INDEX

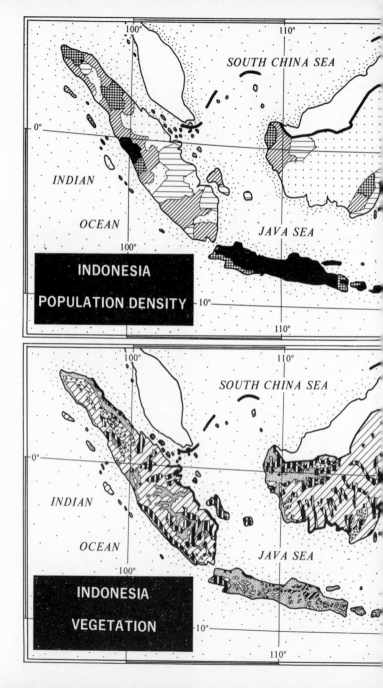

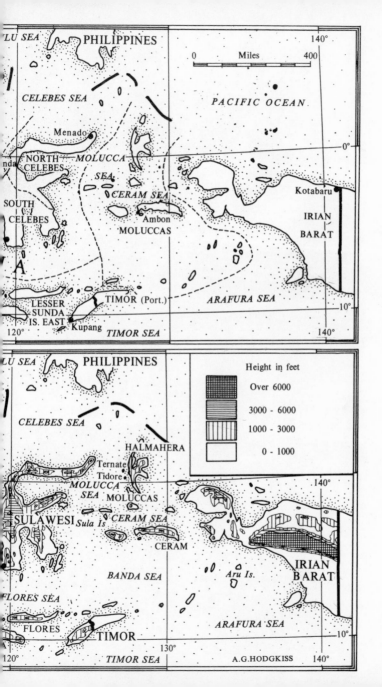